TRIBAL DEVELOPMENT IN INDIA

TRIBAL DEVELOPMENT IN INDIA

WITH SPECIAL REFRENCE TO ORISSA

Dr. Taradatt

GYAN PUBLISHING HOUSE
New Delhi-110 002

Published from the grant provided by the Ministry of Tribal Affairs, Government of India

TRIBAL DEVELOPMENT IN INDIA
(With Special Reference to Orissa)

ISBN : 9788121207706

Published in 2015 in India by
Gyan Publishing House
5, Ansari Road,
New Delhi-110 002

Dedicated

To

Pranab Prakash (Raja)

Contents

Abbreviations

BDO	=	Block Development Officer
DRDA	=	District Rural Development Agency
DTDP	=	Dispersed Tribal Area Development Project
HS	=	High School
ICDP	=	Integrated Child Development Project
IEO	=	Indicators of Economic Development
ITDA	=	Integrated Tribal Development Agency
ITDP	=	Integrated Tribal Development Project
LAMPS	=	Large Size Multi-Purpose Cooperative Society
LPS	=	Lower Primary School
MADA	=	Modified Area Development Approach
PLC	=	Project Level Committee
RDTA	=	Report on Development of Tribal Areas
SC	=	Scheduled Caste
SCA	=	Special Central Assistance
ST	=	Scheduled Tribe
TAC	=	Tribes Advisory Council
TD	=	Tribal Development
TSP	=	Tribal Sub Plan
UIP	=	Universal Immunization Programme
UPS	=	Upper Primary School
UT	=	Union Territory
WGR	=	Working Group Report

Preface

The socio-economic development of Communities designated as 'Tribes' through development interventions has been a major challenge before the framers of the Constitution, planners and field administrators after the independence. The Colonial Administration had practised a policy of non-intervention and kept these communities segregated describing them in contradistinction to the rest of the society in terms of their traditions, religion, culture and social ethos, etc. Even after independence, the anthropologist led school of tribal development called for a minimum intervention pleading that construction of roads in tribal areas will enhance their vulnerability to exploitation and modern education will destroy their culture, social cohesiveness, etc. The anthropologists had suggested that any development of these communities should be along the lines of their genius and the few programmes to be implemented in the tribal areas should have a 'tribal touch' or 'tribal bias". Indeed, the communities which should have been served with far more attention became victims of too much display of romanticism in the name of preserving tribal art, craft, culture, tradition, etc. by the Social Anthropologists, who preferred 'isolation' over 'assimilation'. "Anthropology for you and History for us" became the ultimate expression of their arrogance.

Well aware of the segregative practices of the past, the framers of our Constitution called for integration of tribal communities into the national mainstream expeditiously. The Constitution envisaged a unique scheme to bring these communities up to a level on a par with the rest of the society through welfare measures, development intervention, political empowerment and protective measures, simultaneously. The Colonial hangover, and romantic mindsets of some leaders, anthropologists and administrators, however, affected the process of assimilation and implementation of developmental programmes for many years, even after independence. Enough attention could not be given for development of infrastructure and education in tribal areas despite the national policies recognising the weaknesses in these key and critical areas and pledging correctives. Nevertheless, it would be grossly unfair to conclude that nothing substantial was achieved, although no one can deny that a lot more remains to be done to bring the tribal people to the levels of their non-tribal counterparts.

The vitiating atmosphere due to too much of politics has made the task of developing tribal areas and people inhabiting those places increasingly complicated. The induced and continuing tendency in some intellectuals, leaders and non-governmental organisations to underline and magnify the so-called conflicts between the interests of tribal and non-tribal people seem to be doing more damage to the process of integration and development. The 'protection and development' of tribal people has become a slogan of publicity and fabulous source of livelihood for many!

This book is an assessment of a development functionary who has no claim to knowing the best possible approach to tribal development. The analysis is within the framework of tribal development strategies and schemes as conceived by the national planners and also counts on his personal experience.

I Convey my gratitude to Prof. P.K. Nayak, Director Tribal and Harijan Training cum Research Institute, (Thrti), Bhubneswar, Dr. P.K. Mohanty, Joint Director, Ministry of Tribal Affairs, Government of India, Dr. A.C. Sahoo, Officer on Special Duty, Thrti, Bhubneswar and Sri Prabhat Mahapatra, Deputy Director, Gopabandhu Academy of Administration, Bhubneswar who have taken pains to go through the manuscript besides inspiring me to write the book. But for the enthusiasm of Sri Amit Garg of Gyan Publishing House, New Delhi, the book would not have been published in the present form. I thank the young book-loving entrepreneur. Finally, I would be lacking in my duties if I fail to thank the Government of Orissa for affording me an opportunity to work as a Director, Tribal Welfare for a couple of years which exposed me intimately to the subject. The State Government was also kind enough to give me a brief assignment in the State Training Academy as if to complete the task initiated years back.

New Delhi
1.8.2001

Taradatt

PART-I
ASPECTS, PROSPECTS AND ISSUES

1

Introduction

The term "Tribe" has been derived from its Latin root "tribes" meaning thereby "a social group". The Oxford Dictionary explains tribe as a "group of people in a primitive or barbarous stage of development acknowledging the authority of a chief and usually regarding themselves as having a common ancestor" (Fuchs, 1977:23). The Tribes in India have been described in different ways by colonial administrators dealing with census matters and by anthropologists.

Characteristics of A Tribe

The colonial administrators dealing with census matters described tribes under the religious heading "Animism" despite some differences. Baines, Census Commissioner, 1891, considered the distinction between tribal people, who were Hinduized and those that followed their tribal form of religion as futile. However, he termed the latter as forest tribes using the word "Tribal Animism" to differentiate them from others. Enthroven, Census Superintendent, Bombay, 1901, referred to the practical difficulty of distinguishing the so-called animists from others, who formed regular Hindu castes. Likewise, Resley did not find any contrasting division between Animism and Hinduism. Gait, Census Commissioner, 1911, almost endorsed the views of Resley. Following the same pattern Tallants, Census Superintendent, Orissa-Bihar, 1921, realised difficulties in differentiating tribes from Hindus in recording Animism as tribal religion. Sediwick, Census Superintendent, Maharashtra,1921, came across a similar situation and suggested that Animism as a religion should be abandoned. Hutton, Census Commissioner, 1931, preferred to change the religious division of Animism into that of Tribal Religion. He used the term "Tribal" in contradiction to Hindu, Muslim and Christian, etc. (Ghurye, 1959 : 1-19).

Common Characteristics of Tribes

Most of the anthropologists have found certain common characteristics such as smallness, isolation, common dialect, common occupational practices, feeling of belonging to a group, own customary laws, etc., among the Indian tribal groups, which distinguish them from others.

Prof. Dube (1977:2) emphasizes the distinction of tribes in the sense that their roots in the soil date back to a very early period; they live in the relative isolation of the hills and the forests; their sense of history is shallow, for among them, the remembered history beyond five to six generations tends to get merged in mythology; they have a low level of techno-economic development; in terms of their cultural ethos, language, institutions, belief and customs, they stand out from the other sections of the society and if they are not egalitarian, they are at least non-hierarchic.

Differentiating Factors

Dr. Naik (Vidyarthi, (ed.) 1984 : 71-72) differentiates the tribal groups from others on account of least functional interdependence within the community; lack of understanding about the full import of monetary economics; primitive means of exploiting natural resources; under-developed stage of economy; multifarious economic pursuits; comparative geographic isolation from other people; common dialect with regional variations; political unity under a common tribal authority; least desire to change and customary laws, which are different from those of majority communities.

According to Bailey (1960:263), tribes can be distinguished from Caste Hindus due to the fact that they live in the hills; they are not Hindus but animists; they are economically backward; they are autochthonous; and they speak tribal languages.

Niharranjan Ray (1972) suggests that the Sanskrit term *Jana* refers to primitive communities of the autochthonous people like the Savaras, the Kullutas, the Kohas, the Bhillas, the Khasas, the Kinnars and a countless number of many others of ancient time, whom today we know as 'tribes'. Territories inhabited by these communities came to be known as Janapadas with the passage of time. There are frequent references in the ancient classical literature describing such territories as *Atatvik Rajya*, *Manikantara* (great forest region), and *pratyantaradesa* (frontier regions). Assimilation of these communities with the other sections of the society has been a slow but a steady process. This indeed, shaped the socio-cultural history of India.

Analyzing the facts about tribes, against their historical background and views of the colonial administrators and anthropologists, Prof. Ghurye (Ibid) found it appropriate to describe them as the imperfectly integrated classes of Hindu society, who could be designated as the tribal classes of Hindu society, for the sake of convenience. Considering the strong tendencies of upward mobility among the various castes and classes in India, Prof. Srinivas (1966) seems to be suggesting the same thing while talking of 'Sanskritisation' in the process of social change in modern India. Deliberately or not the Colonial Administrators dealing with Census matters seem to have ignored the vital historical and traditional links among the various social groups while defining the various classes described in the ancient literature-Adivasis (original settlers); Girijans (hill-dwellers); Vanyajati (forest caste); Adimjati (primitive caste); etc., differently. The vast majority of anthropologists, both from the West and Eest, followed suit.

Tribes as Notified in the Constitution

The problem as to which sections of the population belong to the tribes has been decided finally under Article 342 of the Constitution of India, according to which the President may, after consultation with the Governor, specify the tribes or tribal communities, which shall, for the purposes of the Constitution, be deemed to be "Scheduled Tribes" (ST) in relation to that State. Clause (2) of the Article in question, further states that Parliament may by law include in or exclude from the list of Scheduled Tribes specified in a notification under clause (1), any tribe or tribal community. According to the Scheduled Tribe Order (Constitution Order 9), 1950, read with the amendment of 1976, 476 communities in all, have been identified as Scheduled Tribes.

Tribal Population in India

According to 1991 Census, 8.01 per cent of the total population in India consists of tribals. In addition to the predominantly Tribal States of Nagaland, Meghalaya, Arunachal Pradesh and Mizoram, which constitute 3.75 per cent of the country's geographical area, tribal sub plan area and pockets comprise about 15 per cent of India's total area. Tribal population and area covered under Tribal Sub Plan including pockets of tribal concentrations (1991 census) are indicated in Table 1.1.

Table 1.1

Tribal Population in Sub Plan Area

Sl. No.	State/UT	Area (Sq. Km.)	Population (in millions)	ST Population (in million)	Percentage of STs
1.	A.P	276754	66.51	4.20	6.31
2.	Assam	78523	22.41	2.87	12.82
3.	Bihar	94162	64.63	0.58	0.90
4.	Chhattisgarh	135100	17.61	5.72	32.47
5.	Gujarat	195984	41.31	6.16	14.92
6.	H.P.	55673	5.17	0.22	4.22
7.	Jharkhand	79714	21.84	6.04	27.65
8.	Karnatak	191773	44.98	1.92	4.26
9.	Kerala	38864	229.10	0.32	1.10
10.	M.P.	307041	46.47	9.72	20.92
11.	Maharashtra	307762	78.94	7.32	9.27
12.	Manipur	22356	1.84	0.63	34.41
13.	Orissa	155842	31.66	7.03	22.21
14.	Rajasthan	332214	44.01	5.47	12.44
15.	Sikkim	7000	0.41	0.09	22.36
16.	Tamil Nadu	130069	55.86	0.57	1.03
17.	Tripura	10477	2.76	0.85	30.95
18.	U.P.	238568	132.07	0.076	0.55
19.	Uttaranchal	55845	7.04	0.21	3.o4
20.	W. B.	87853	68.08	3.80	5.59
21.	A&N Island	8293	0.28	0.003	9.54
22.	Daman & Diu	3813	0.01	0.0011	11.54

(Census, 1991)

Tribal Situation During the Colonial Administration

One of the important characteristics of tribal communities has been its traditional association with a territory. Initially, the community lived on food-gathering and hunting in the areas in its command. As the pressure of population grew and the community acquired new skills of agriculture, they cleared forests and brought the land under cultivation. However, the tribal areas remained for a long time outside the land management systems of the Colonial Administration because of inaccessibility. The tribal communities developed their own traditions of management of land, which could be placed in three broad categories, i.e., community land, land belonging to a clan and individual holding.

As the Colonial Rule consolidated its position and introduced new systems of land management, some of the tribal areas were also integrated with it. Still, the policy of treating some of the tribal areas as excluded and partially excluded areas helped in the continuance of the traditional tribal system. The policy of non-intervention in the affairs of the tribals, however, kept them in the atmosphere of isolation, untouched by the civilization of the plains. The Dhebar Commission aptly quoted Dr. J.H. Hutton, a member from the Indian Civil Service, giving light to the effect of the Colonial Administration on the tribals in the following words:

> "Far from being of immediate benefit to the primitive tribes, the establishment of British Rule in India did most of them much more harm than good..... It may be said that the early days of British administration did very great detriment to the economic position of tribes through ignorance and neglect of their rights and customs... many changes have been caused incidentally by the penetration of the tribal country, the opening of communications, the protection of forests and the establishment of schools to say nothing of the openings given in this way to Christian Missions. Many of the results of these changes have caused acute discomfort to tribes".

The efforts of British administration to introduce a system of legal and enforceable rights and new pattern of land settlement brought in a commercial orientation towards the land as a resource. Illiterate tribals obviously could not understand the new system of law and courts and in the process lost a large portion of their land. The new legal system started superseding the traditional customs gradually and the tribals could not withstand the pressure of outsiders. In various tribal regions, the opening of new channels of communication increased the volume of non-tribal immigration which was further intensified with the opening of mines for commercial exploitation. Under such a situation of economic, social and cultural threats, a series of tribal revolts took place during the 18th and 19th centuries. Regulation 1 of 1796 ultimately recognized the rights of tribals in Rajmahal hills tracts, withholding the operation of regular laws and jurisdiction of the ordinary courts. The tract was administered by the Collector, making his own rules for the conduct of the affairs of tribals, after taking into account their customary laws. As a result of the "Col Rebellion" of 1831 and "Santhal Rebellion" of 1855, similar arrangements were made to protect the interests of tribals through various Regulations and Acts (Ghurye, 1959: 74-76). Unfortunately, no positive attempts were made to assimilate the tribals into the mainstream, though incidentally some changes did take place, due to opening of communication and penetration of some Christian Missionaries into the tribal communities.

Constitutional Provisions for the Uplift of Tribals

Despite a strong tendency of perceiving tribes in contradistinction to the rest of the Indian social structure, an indepth study of Indian sociology shows that interaction between the various segments of the society has been continuous. Over a period of time, tribal groups have succeeded in establishing claim to "Kshatriyahood" and elements of tribal rituals and social life have found their ways into higher Hinduism (Srinivas, 1966:153-55). Nevertheless, the framers of Indian Constitution were fully aware of the socio-economic backwardness of tribes and the necessity to fully assimilate them into the main body at a greater pace. Special provisions were thus made relating to the protection and promotion of their interests in the field of : (a) Political Representation; (b) Representation in Government Posts and Services; (c) Socio-Economic Development; and (d) Legal and Administrative Support. The provisions in brief are as follows:

Political Representation

Provisions for political representation of Scheduled Tribes in the Union and State Legislatures under Articles 330 and 332 of the Constitution have to be in proportion to their population.

Representation in Posts and Services

Article 335 of the Constitution enjoins on the Union Government and States to take the claims of Scheduled Tribes into consideration in the making of appointments to Government services and posts.

Socio-economic Development

Article 46 of the Constitution makes it obligatory on the State to promote with special care, the educational and economic interests of weaker sections of the people, in particular, Scheduled Tribes, and to protect them from social injustice and all forms of exploitation.

Legal and Administrative Support

Considering the large concentration of tribes in Bihar, Orissa and Madhya Pradesh States, provisions have been made under Article 164 of the Constitution to keep a Minister in charge of tribal welfare, in these States. Article 338 provides for the constitution of a National Commission: to investigate and monitor all matters relating to the safeguards provided for the Scheduled Tribes; to participate and advise on the planning process of socio-economic development of the Scheduled Tribes; to inquire into specific complaints with respect to the deprivation of rights and safeguards of Scheduled Tribes; to present to the President reports upon the working of safeguards deemed fit by the Commission; to make recommendation regarding the measures to be taken by the Union or States for welfare, protection and socio-economic development and to discharge any other function in relation to the protection, welfare and development of Scheduled Tribes.

Under Article 339, the President is required to appoint a Commission to report on the administration of the scheduled areas and the welfare of the Scheduled Tribes. Article 342 envisages notification of Scheduled Tribes through presidential order in consultation with the States concerned and authority of the parliament to make law for inclusion or exclusion of any community from the list of Scheduled Tribes specified in the presidential notification.

The fifth schedule of the Constitution applies to the administration of the scheduled areas and Scheduled Tribes of the States other than Assam, Meghalaya, Tripura and Mizoram, which are to be governed by provisions under the sixth schedule of the Constitution. As per provisions under Article 244 (1), the Governor of each State having scheduled areas therein, shall annually or whenever so required by the President, make a report regarding the administration of scheduled areas in that State and the executive power of the Union shall extend to the giving of directions to the States as to the administration of the said areas .

Part "B" of the fifth schedule explains the procedure to be adopted in the administration of the scheduled areas and Scheduled Tribes. Each State having scheduled areas has to have a "Tribes Advisory Council" (TAC). The duty of the TAC is to advise the Governor on matters relating to the advancement of tribals in the State as may be referred to them by the Governor.

The fifth schedule of the Constitution gives sweeping powers to the Governor for the administration of scheduled areas. He may, by public notification, withhold operation of any particular Act of the parliament or the State Legislature in the scheduled area or any part thereof. The Governor may also make regulations in consultation with the TAC, for peace and good government of any area in the State, which is for the time being a scheduled area.

The sixth schedule of the Constitution enables the Governors of Assam, Meghalaya, Manipur and Tripura to form Autonomous Districts, Autonomous Regions, District Councils and Regional Councils with adequate legal, administrative and financial powers for the administration of justice, respecting the needs, customary laws and practices of the tribals of the north eastern States.

The first proviso to Article 275 (1) of the Constitution, provides for release of Central Assistance from the Consolidated Fund of India to meet the cost of such schemes of development as may be undertaken for strengthening of administration in the scheduled areas of the States.

This study seeks to analyze the principles, policy issues, trends and approaches of Tribal Development in the post-independence period, taking into account the historical background of tribal communities, as discussed above. It will critically examine the "gains" and "setbacks" of "Protective Legislation" and "Development Intervention" in retrospect and prospect. In addition to reviewing the relevant literature on the subject, the book draws from the author's own experience in the process of making some recommendations for further refinement in the tribal development administration.

2

Tribal Development after Independence

The Scheduled Tribes, who have been so designated under Article 342 of the Constitution are broadly composed of 250 tribal groups speaking about 105 languages and 225 subsidiary languages spread over the length and breadth of India, concentrated mostly in the hilly and forest regions (WGR 1980-85:1). Despite differences of race, language, culture and belief, there are certain broad similarities among the mutually divergent tribal groups in the sense that they have been less developed, inward-looking, subsistence-oriented, tradition- bound and self-governed. It has naturally been a complex and uphill task to translate the Constitutional goals into action and make them catch up with the non-tribals in the race for social, political and economic prosperity. The attempts made so far to achieve the goals can be discussed under two broad heads: Development Intervention and Protective Legislation.

Development Intervention : Planned Initiatives

The planned development intervention in Tribal India is essentially a post-independence phenomenon. It envisages a shift in the principles from 'isolationism' to 'assimilation' into the mainstream of the national culture. It envisions further shifts from welfare and growth oriented economic development to human resources and equity centred development.

Tribal Development Prior to the Introduction of the Tribal Sub Plan (TSP) Approach

The socio-economic development of tribals had its humble beginning right from the first five year plan (1951-56), when the funding for the tribal development programme constituted one per cent of the total plan outlay. The tribal communities like the rest of the nation were expected to participate in the planned economic development on terms of equality. A programme for community development was initiated during the first five year plan through 56 community development projects, which covered the entire country by end of the second plan. The concept of community development programme was equally applied to the tribal areas. However, considering the operational difficulties due to poor communication network and negligible institutional infrastructure, etc; the community development programme in tribal areas was supplemented initially (in 1954) by some (43) special multipurpose tribal development projects and subsequently (during the second five year plan) by introducing the concept of the Tribal Development (TD) block.

A review during the third five year plan revealed that the TD block programme did not have the desired impact. It was therefore decided to add a phase of five years to the TD blocks already started and not to extend the geographical area (Report on the Development of Tribal Areas (RDTA), 1981:13). The weakness of Tribal Development programmes became evident when the implementation took a schematic form notwithstanding conceptual comprehensiveness and all inclusiveness. Despite protective legislation, the process of land alienation started weakening the economic base of tribals due to lack of coordination between the regulatory and developmental branches of the administration.

In 1959, a Committee was set up under the chairmanship of Elwin Verrier to study the progress of development in selected tribal areas throughout the country. The Committee submitted its findings (Report of the Committee on Special Multi-Purpose Tribal Blocks) in 1960, suggesting a 'tribal bias' or 'tribal touch' to the policy and schemes relating to tribal development and expansion of properly adapted developmental schemes during the third five year plan.

In pursuance of the provisions under Article 339 the "Scheduled Areas and Scheduled Tribe Commission" (known as Dhebar Commission), was set up in April 1960. In its comprehensive report (1961) while recording the gains of development intervention, the Commission pointed to the unsatisfactory pace of tribal development due to inadequate investment together with protective measures. Recommendations were made for comprehensive legislation and simple administrative structure for the development of tribal areas.

Another review of the "Tribal development" was taken up by the Shilu A. Committee in 1969 (Report of the Study Team on Tribal Development

Programme). The Committee found TD blocks inadequate to deal with the complex problems of development in addition to drawing attention to the non-implementation of the recommendations made by the Dhebar Commission. It called for vigorous action to prepare tribal development programmes allocating resources, commensurate with the size of the problem and overall national development efforts (RDTA, 1981:14).

The fourth five year plan (1969-74) envisaged a shift in the development intervention from the Area Development approach to the Beneficiary Oriented schemes. Tribal development agencies were established as Pilot Projects towards the end of the plan period.

The Tribal Sub Plan (TSP) Approach

The continued socio-economic backwardness of tribal communities remained a key point of discussion on the eve of the fifth five year plan. Despite some gains and advancement by some of the tribal communities, the setbacks highlighted by Dhebar Commission and Shilu A. Committee had remained uncorrected. Installation of mining and industrial complexes in the mineral rich tribal areas amounted to little benefits to the tribals.

Salient Features

Thus, in the fifth plan, a distinct approach for development of tribal communities was worked out. The Strategy outlined as TSP approach contained the following salient features:

1. Identification of States with tribal majority blocks and their constitution into the Integrated Tribal Development Projects (ITDPs), with a view to adopting therein an integrated and projectised approach for development.
2. Preparation of integrated project report for each ITDP keeping in view the natural resources of the regions and the skills, aptitudes and needs of the population.
3. Creation of appropriate administrative structure in tribal areas and adoption of appropriate personnel policies.
4. Quantification of financial resources from out of the State and Central plans for tribal areas and tribal people broadly corresponding to the tribal population percentage in the total population of the State (Tribal Development in the Fifth Plan, 1982).

Enhanced Budget Allocation in the Five Year Plans

The investment towards tribal development programmes experienced a sharp enhancement from 0.5 per cent in the preceding plan period to

3.01 per cent of the total plan outlay, during the fifth plan period as a result of the TSP approach. The next two plans emphasised explicitly the poverty alleviation programmes and witnessed substantial investment in tribal development with a view to ensuring both, material and non material benefits to tribal communities.

The fifth five year plan is a landmark in the history of tribal development administration and a harbinger of new aspirations and expectations. The areas with high tribal concentration were identified and the flow of funds was quantified. The administration of tribal development was streamlined with the emergence of the Integrated Tribal Development Projects (ITDPs), as the units of administration in the tribal sub plan area.

The sixth plan (1980-85), carried forward the policy and approaches evolved during the 5th plan period and sharpened the implementation. Smaller pockets having more than 50 per cent of the population belonging to the Scheduled Tribes, were identified for comprehensive coverage under various poverty alleviation schemes and tribal development projects. The tribal pockets which remained excluded from ITDPs, were covered under Modified Area Development Approach (MADA).

There has been no change in the strategy during the seventh and subsequent five year plans. The efforts have been to consolidate the gains under the TSP approach and to orient them to the targeted groups. Since ITDPs and MADA covered 75 per cent of the tribal population in the country, a Cluster approach was formulated to cover the smaller pockets of tribal population, in addition to the Dispersed Tribal Development Projects (DTDP) for the tribals still remaining uncovered.

The TSP approach was conceived in 1974-75 noting the crucial fact that an incisive approach to the tribal problems was necessary in terms of their geographic and demographic concentration for a faster development of this community. The tribal areas in the country were classified under three broad categories:

(a) States and Union Territories (UTs) having a majority of tribal population;

(b) States and UTs having substantial tribal population in specific administrative units such as blocks and tehsils; and

(c) States and UTs having dispersed tribal population (WGR 1985-90:1).

The tribal majority States and UTs like Arunachal Pradesh, Meghalaya, Nagaland, Mizoram, Lakshadweep and Dadra & Nagar Haweli did not need a Tribal Sub Plan, as the entire plan of these States and UTs was primarily meant for the tribal population.

The TSP approach was implemented in the second category of States and UTs after identifying Blocks with more than 50 per cent tribal population. It was decided to accept area development approach with focus on individual tribal families. The strategy involved 18 States and UTs. A similar approach was followed in respect of States and UTs having dispersed tribal population.

The Working Group recorded the goals of the sixth five year plan as follows: (a) Raising the productivity levels in the fields of agriculture, animal husbandry, forestry, cottage industry, etc., so as to create an economic impact of an order which will enable a targeted number of families in the TSP areas to cross the poverty line; (b) Developing human resources and upgrading education; (c) Development of adequate infrastructure; (d) Elimination of exploitation of tribals in the fields of alienation of land, money lending, debt, bondage, trade, excise, forests, etc. (WGR, 1980-85:15).

Financial Framework under TSP Approach

The TSP approach envisages integrated development of tribal communities. Irrespective of their sources of funding, all the programmes and projects under this strategy are required to operate in unison to achieve the goal of bringing the tribals up to the level of the rest of the country. The investment flows from four sources: (1) State plan; (2) Central Ministries; (3) Special Central Assistance (SCA) and (4) Institutional finance.

In addition to the sources of investment mentioned above, the first proviso to Article 275(1) of the Constitution makes it obligatory on the part of the Union Government to provide financial allocation from the Consolidated Fund, to raise the level of administration in TSP areas and implementation of the schemes meant for tribals. Occasional financial assistance is also given by the Union Government for development of essential institutional infrastructure including residential accommodation and compensatory allowance for the Government functionaries working in the remote tribal areas.

Another important element of the TSP approach is non-divertibility and non-lapseability of TSP funds. Diversion of outlays quantified and earmarked for the Tribal Sub Plan is not permitted. Similarly, unspent amount of the SCA is allowed to be carried over to the next financial year without any fear of being lapsed.

Administrative Structures for *TSP Approach*

Although the TSP approach has been conceived at the national level,the responsibility for its implementation is left to the States and UTs with the role of the Union Government as a guide. It is natural that different States and UTs have tried to implement the TSP approach with some variations, without tempering with the basic conceptual framework. The administrative framework for the implementation of the TSP approach, by and large, is as follows:

(a) Integrated Tribal Development Projects (ITDP)

The most important unit of administration in the TSP approach at the district level is the ITDP, which has taken the agency form in some States ie.Andhra Pradesh and Orissa, where they are known by the name: Integrated Tribal Development Agencies (ITDAs). The ITDP/ITDA consists of a number of contiguous blocks within a district with more than 50% of the population being tribals and is responsible for planning, monitoring and implementation of the tribal development projects and welfare schemes. ITDPs/ITDAs, which are headed by Project Administrators, function under the overall supervision of the Collector, the head of the district administration. The tribal welfare schemes and developmental programmes in non-ITDP/ITDA areas are however, implemented by the Panchayat Samities known as the Blocks.

(b) Regional Administrative Bodies

In order to bridge the physical administrative gulf, some of the TSP states have gone for another unit of administrative structure headed by the Development Commissioner at the regional level.In the States of Maharashtra and Rajasthan, Additional Commissioners are in charge of the regional bodies with independent territorial and functional jurisdictions. Certain States like Madhya Pradesh and Bihar have created Regional Development Authorities with a view to decentralising the functions and securing better coordination at the project level.

(c) Administrative Set-up at the State Level

The structure of the Tribal development administration varies from State to State. In some States, the policy making body is directly headed by the Chief Minister, while other states have a Committee comprised of ministers and officials in the nature of a Steering Committee (WGR, 1980-85:34-35). There has to be an independent minister in charge of the

Tribal Welfare Department in the States of Madhya Pradesh, Orissa and Bihar as per provisions under Article 164 of the Constitution. In all the TSP states, Tribal Research Institutes have been established to advise the Government on matters relating to the planning, implementation, monitoring and evaluation of the tribal development programmes and training of the personnel involved in the field administration.

(d) Tribes Advisory Council (TAC)

As stated earlier, each State having scheduled areas has to establish a TAC as per provisions laid down under the 5th Schedule of the Constitution. The TAC headed by the Chief Minister of the State concerned, is required to advise on matters pertaining to welfare and advancement of Scheduled Tribes in the State.

(e) Role of Governor

As envisaged in the fifth schedule to the Constitution, the Governor of each State having scheduled areas is required to submit a report to the President annually regarding administration of such areas in the State. Special provisions on administration and control of the tribal areas and scheduled tribes under article 244(1) of the Constitution confer wide powers on the Governors to make regulations for peace and good government, which are crucial for tribal development.

(f) Administration of Tribal Development at the Centre

The Constitution provides for a delicate amalgam of the responsibilities to the Union Government relating to protection, administration and welfare of the tribals. Different Ministries in the Centre are expected to perform specific functions in consultation with the States. The National Committee on the Development of Backward Areas (1981) suggested for the establishment of Tribal Development Department in stead of a division under the Home Ministry. Accordingly, the Union Ministry of Tribal Affairs is in charge of Tribal development at present.

(g) National Commission for the Scheduled Tribes

Article 338 of the Constitution calls for the appointment of a National Commission by the President of India.It is the duty of the National Commission to investigate matters relating to the safeguards provided for the scheduled tribes under the Constitution and report to the president upon the working of those safeguards at such intervals as the President may direct and the President has to cause all such reports to be laid before each house of the Parliament. At present, the Commission consists of seven members including a Chairman and a Vice-Chairman.

Protective Legislation for Tribals

Promotion of developmental programmes in a planned manner along with the protection of tribal interests through legislative measures has been the two dimensional approach accepted for the development of tribals in free India. The Constitution specifically requires the States to promote the economic and educational interests of the tribes and to protect them from social injustice and exploitation. Special powers have been conferred on the Governors of the States having scheduled areas to pass regulations in regard to restriction on transfer and allotment of land and money lending business. The Governor may also by notification withhold the operation of general laws passed by the parliament or the State Legislature in scheduled areas considering the interests of tribals. The protective legislation covers mainly the following aspects:

Land Alienation

More than 90 per cent of the tribals are dependent on agriculture and allied activities (RDTA, 1981:49). A number of social and religious rituals of tribals are connected with land, which is the only tangible asset with them. All the expert bodies have been unanimous in calling for measures to prevent land alienation of tribals..

By and large, legislations and regulations have been passed by States to ensure that tribal land does not pass on to the non-tribal, illegally and fraudulently. Unfortunately, lack of awareness about the laws in respect of alienation of land among the tribals, cumbersome processes and loopholes have resulted in whittling down significantly the effect of these legislations. A study conducted by the Department of Rural Development, Government of India, shows that of the total tribal land alienated, about 40 per cent was by way of sale, 25 per cent by way of mortgage, lease and remaining 10 per cent by other modes.In the modes other than land acquisition, 80 per cent of the land had gone to the non-tribal (WGR,1990-95 : 35).

Money Lending and Relief from Indebtedness

Continuous indebtedness is one of the main indicators of poverty, which has been a serious problem among the tribals largely due to the imbalance between income and minimum consumption requirements and lack of resources for carrying on gainful activity and employment. A sample study done by the Planning Commission in selected ITDPs, reveals that the indebtedness among the tribals increased from 14.4 per cent in 1975-76 to 33.77 per cent in 1982-83. The debt liability per household increased from Rs. 419/ in 1975-76 to Rs. 818/ in 1982-83. The tribals borrowed money from both institutional and non-institutional sources. Seventy-two percent of the tribals were indebted to non-institutional sources including shop-keepers, friends, relatives, etc. while four percent of the tribals were indebted to institutional sources, both banks and co-operatives (WGR, 1990-95: 37).

Most of the TSP States and UTs have passed laws and regulations to regulate the business of money lending and relief from debt. Simultaneous steps have also been taken to establish institutional sources of credit at reasonable rates of interest for various self employment ventures, productive and consumption purposes.

Access to Forests

The tribal communities have had a symbiotic relationship with forests, where they lived for a long period of their history in relative isolation. Even today, they draw their sustenance from the forests in the remote areas. Unfortunately, the relationship between the forests and tribals received little attention for a long time. The Working Group on Tribal Development (1990-95 : 40) pointedly referred to this insensitivity in the following words:

> The National Forest Policy, 1952, did not take into account the relationship between tribals and forests and almost completely ignored the symbiosis in this relationship. Even the claims of tribals in forests, which they had enjoyed for generations were subordinated to the National interest and were reduced to mere rights and concessions. The implementation of the policy resulted in the over-exploitation of forests in the absence of any framework for increasing the area under the forests. Diversion of forest land to non-forest purposes was permitted liberally up to 1980, when The Forest Conservation Act had to be passed to prevent the dwindling of the forest base further in the country. The problems of tribals, who depended on the forests in many ways, were however, accentuated till the National Forest Policy was modified recognising the symbiotic relationship of tribals with the forests in 1988.

The National Commission on Agriculture (1976) found the potential of revolutionising the economy of tribals in minor forest produce and called for nationalisation of forest produce with a view to check exploitation of tribals and to ensure a fair price for primary tribal collectors of forest produce. This facilitated formation of Tribal Development Cooperative Corporations in States having sizable tribal population for the procurement and marketing of minor forest produce at protective and remunerative prices, through the primary cooperative societies consisting of tribals or directly. Through this process, elimination of exploitation by middlemen has been achieved to a degree.

Considering the recommendations of the Working Group on the development of Scheduled Tribes during the 7th Five Year Plan, Government of India has set up the Tribal Marketing Development Federation of India Ltd (TRIFED) as an apex body of state tribal development corporations at the national level in 1987.This body now helps in procurement and marketing of forest produce.

The deficiency in the old National Forest Policy was removed to a large extent in the new Forest Policy of 1988, which gives due recognition to the symbiotic relationship between the tribals and the forests by stipulating: involvement of tribals in the protection, regeneration and development of forests; replacement of contractors by tribal co-operatives to avoid degradation of forest; protection, regeneration and optimum collection of minor forest produce along with institutional arrangement for the marketing of such produce; integrated area development programmes to meet the needs of the tribal economy in and around the forest areas (WGR, 1990-95 : 40).

The new policy also recognises the rights and concessions enjoyed by the tribals traditionally in addition to accepting the fact of shifting cultivation and needs to develop the forest villages in the same manner as of the revenue villages.

3

Expert Committee Reports on Tribal Development

A number of Expert Committees and Commissions have been constituted by Government of India and as well as by Planning Commission to evaluate the impact of constitutional/legal provisions and various programmes directed at socio-economic uplift of tribals and development of the Scheduled Areas. It would be of interest to discuss some of these reports in brief to appreciate the results of the planned initiatives, along with the assessment and recommendations made by the experts from time to time

Report of the Committee on Special Multipurpose Tribal Blocks

The Committee headed by Verrier Elwin constituted by the Ministry of Home Affairs, Government of India in May, 1959 to study the functioning of the Special Multipurpose Tribal Blocks furnished its report on 30th March, 1960. The Committee's terms of reference were: (i) to study the the working of the Special Multi-Purpose Tribal Development Block and (ii) to advise the Government of India on how to implement the intensive development programme of the Blocks more effectively and give the programme a proper tribal bias.

The Committee was not impressed with the development projects in Special Multipurpose Tribal Blocks, which according to its report did not conform to the actual needs of tribal communities. The Committee pleaded for a self induced development of the tribal people along the lines of their own genius, laying emphasis on their traditions, arts, religion, culture, rights on the land and forests, restriction on outsiders to enter into tribal territory, working through their social and cultural institutions and evaluating quality of human culture without judging results by statistics or the amount of money spent under various programmes. The fundamental approach to the tribal development according to the report should be to avoid over administration of tribal areas which invariably takes place by implementing a large number of schemes like communication, medical facilities, improved agriculture, etc. The recommendations with regard to the approach towards tribal development and to implement schemes given by the Expert Committee are as follows:

Recommendations of the Committee

(A) General Approach

Traditionalism in Growth : Development of tribal people should be encouraged along the lines of their own genius and traditions without imposing unfamiliar elements of development. The tribals should not be told to adopt a way of life which is unsuited to their economy. This may result in tribals despising their own arts, social and political institutions, etc. They should not be asked to adopt practice, which do not go hand in hand with their own genius. Any form of monetary incentives will injure them in their organic growth. They should not be over persuaded by Blocks through propaganda and education to do things hampering their natural growth from within. Uprooting them from their traditional life will amount to loss of self- reliance.

The rights of tribals in land and adjustment of forest laws to tribal conditions are as necessary as any expensive schemes of development for their successful implementation.

The tribal communities should be served by building up a team of their own people instead of introducing too many outsiders into tribal territory. The tribal areas should not be over administered with multiplicity of schemes as tribal people are not capable of absorbing several items simultaneously. Instead of wasting a lot of energy on non-essentials like social education, construction of roads, etc., attention should be paid exclusively on agriculture and public health.

Social Education : Social education should consist of only 2 or 3 items. Rural arts and crafts should be considered the essential industries. The most characteristic systems of natural tribal education are destroyed by our educational programmes. They would succeed better accepting the old institution as allies and not as rivals and work through them. The indigenous institutions are being killed by development programmes which is not healthy.

Programme Implementation with Tribal Touch : Success or failure of programmes should not be estimated by expenditure and statistics like enrolment in schools, area brought under cultivation and horticulture, etc. The undue emphasis on expenditure reverses the original spirit of the community programme. Undue material and financial assistance to motivate the people may prove counter productive for the growth of community. In agricultural field the danger of giving free gifts (inputs for improved agriculture) to the tribals should be avoided as money and materials destroy the community spirit.

No unrealistic promise should be made while introducing and implementing development programmes. The officers and staff serving tribal areas should have the right attitude for working among those communities. The tendency to blame everything on the laziness, the improvidence, the suspiciousness and superstition of the tribal people should be avoided.

The programmes of development in tribal areas should have a 'tribal touch' or a 'tribal bias' instead of adopting stereotyped plans which are suitable for development of non-tribal regions. All the development programmes should be adjustable to the culture and religion of tribals and should be looked at through their eyes. We must find out what means most to them recognizing their way of things.

(B) Specific Recommendation Relating to Implementation of Schemes

Special pay should be granted to officials working in the Special Multipurpose Tribal Blocks. Special training of officials should be organised for working in tribal areas and they should not be subjected to frequent transfers. Intensive training should be given to the Culture Officers to be posted to tribal Blocks.

Land Rights : the State Governments should take up as a measure of priority, to survey the tribal areas in order to discover the amount of cultivable land and the extent to which the tribal people have no established rights in the areas they cultivate. This should be followed by vigorous and sincere attempt to establish the rights of tribal people on the land which they have cultivated traditionally. The laws against alienation of tribal land and similar protective measures should be carefully examined in the light of the present situation. The aim should be to ensure that every tribal family gets at least two and a half acres of wet or 5 acres of dry land for cultivation.

Method of Cultivation : No attempt should be made to prohibit shifting cultivation in a hurry as it would cause a drastic disturbance of tribal life; the process of shifting cultivation should be reversed through settled cultivation ultimately if tribal people live on their own prosperous farms at a reasonable distance from their habitations with undisputed rights. The States should set up demonstration farms in the remote places to train and convince the tribals about the profitability of improved agriculture. Terraced cultivation in the hill slopes should be encouraged and facilities of irrigation provided by construction of smaller irrigation projects.

Forest Earnings : The tribals should have direct share in the profits of forests. This can be done by relating wages to profits or reserving really remunerative revenue coupes for allotment to tribal cooperative societies on a fixed offset price allowing substantial margin of profits. Forest should be managed essentially in the interest of tribals who inhabit the areas. Precautions should be taken to avoid hardship to forest villagers arising from demand for their labour at a time when they are themselves engaged in agriculture operation.

Rearing of Animals : The small animals kept by tribals should be upgraded with caution. Introduction of new breeds may not be suitable for the unfamiliar climate and hilly region. Veterinary services should precede an attempt to upgrade the local stock. In order to improve the conditions and to develop milch and draught cattle, cattle-consciousness should be created among the tribals by means of audio-visual units, exhibition etc. The officials to be employed should be mainly selected from the tribal areas and the incentive to improve the condition of their domestic animals should come from the tribals themselves.

Carefully Planned Roads : Roads can be a curse as well as a blessing to the tribal people. They can bring new diseases, moral decline, cultural decadence, money lenders and liquor vendors, etc. They can bring money in and out. Attempts should therefore be made to avoid the adverse effects of road communication. Priority should be given to construct class–I roads with culverts and causeways, even though these will be bound to be few in number in view of their higher cost. The cost of main roads linking the Blocks with the district headquarters should be charged on the State Budget. Since the tribal people rarely use the roads and prefer their traditional paths which are shorter, Tribal Block areas should be carefully and imaginatively surveyed to construct class 2 and class 3 roads which will be to their advantage. The resources of State Public Work Departments, Local Boards and Forest Departments should be pooled together for construction and maintenance of roads and contractors should be avoided in execution as far as is humanly possible. It is important to make roads linking entire hills and inaccessible tribal areas with the plains and then to join remote villages with each other.

Provision of Medical Facilities : It is essential to have a survey of the area to ascertain the health problems and thus give priorities to effective development of the programmes. The tribal areas offer unparalleled challenges and opportunities to the doctors and nurses. The medical coverage should be provided by integrating medical relief, maternal and child health care, school health, control of communicable diseases, environmental sanitation, and collection of vital statistics. In the Tribal Blocks, each VLW Circle should be provided with a medicine chest under the charge of the VLW or the local school teacher. The medicine chest should be refilled and maintained properly. Malaria Eradication Programme and scheme for control of communicable diseases should be taken up with greater intensity. Provisions should be made for safe drinking water and health education.

Education Programme : Education programme should be worked out carefully to adjust in such a way as to have well trained tribal officers to develop their own areas. Primary education should be given in the local dialects. It should develop pride in the tribal children of their own history and their leaders. The spirit of self-reliance in the school should be maintained as there is a danger that we make education too cheap in our desire to draw boys and girls to schools. The schools should have agriculture and forestry bias.

Promotion of Tribal Arts : Financial assistance should be made available for Training Centres and Cooperatives for recurring and non-recurring expenditure to promote tribal arts and craft. No schemes of commercial nature should be started in tribal areas unless arrangements for raw materials and marketing are made in advance. Attention should be paid for research on the tribal arts and crafts that already exist. While chalking out programmes, consideration should be given to the locally available raw materials and the marketing facilities. No expensive machines should be introduced. The revival of wood carving has great possibilities both for development and for sale. Attempts to revive weaving in tribal areas should be made everywhere through introduction of fly shuttle loom.

Land Colonisation : The land colonisation scheme almost entirely ignores the desire of tribal people as well as their psychology, religion and social arrangements. The construction of houses using imported materials and plans should be avoided and attempts should be made to improve their existing houses making them fire proof. While it is important to help the poorer people to build better houses, it is equally important that these houses are of a type with which they are familiar.

Credit Cooperative Societies : Effective legislation, administrative enforcement and development of public opinion are essential for liquidation of indebtedness of the tribal people. Besides, an effective system of giving credit for production and consumption purposes and effective promotion of social education among the tribals to encourage thrift to preserve their earnings through small scale saving societies should be encouraged. Primary extension education should precede formation of cooperative societies. Rich and influential people should not be allowed to be members of the cooperatives. Service cooperatives should be formed to serve the largest number of people. The procedure for sanction and disbursement of loan from cooperatives should be simplified to avoid exploitation of innocent tribal people by the unscrupulous money lenders. The sale and marketing of the produce and supply of the tribal people's requirements at reasonable prices should receive special attention through Cooperative organisations.

A careful reading of the Report shows that the Expert Committee has tried to maintain a delicate balance between development intervention and isolation. The assessment and recommendations appear contradictory at times as development is invariably a process of change which may not be possible without breaking the barriers originating from the isolation. Verrier Elwin through this report seems to be conveying his well known notions about the tribal communities and their needs which could be fulfilled by allowing them to remain in the relative isolation of forests ignoring the fact that the relative isolation of tribals relegates them to living in the stone age in their static form. The contradiction also becomes evident when the report praises the intervention by some Christian Missionaries in creating community spirit in some villages of North East India on the one hand and makes critical observations against the Block Officials in Kashipur Block (Orissa) for invoking Hindu Mythological Characters for similar work, on the other. The culture, religions, arts, traditions and social institutions, etc., evolve continuously without being preserved in a static form. The evolution may be described by words like assimilation, integration or Sanskritization.

Report of Scheduled areas and Scheduled Tribes Commission

Article 339 of the Indian Constitution provides that: "The President of India may at any time and shall at the expiration of ten years from the commencement of this Constitution by order appoint a Commission to report on the administration of the Scheduled Areas and the welfare of the Scheduled Tribes in the States. The order may define the composition, power and procedure of the Commission and may contain such incidental or ancillary provisions as the President may consider necessary or desirable". The Scheduled Areas and Scheduled Tribes Commission was appointed by the President of India in pursuance of the constitutional provisions under reference on the 28th of April, 1960.

Areas Investigated

The Commission did an exhaustive exercise with extensive surveys, visited widely all over the tribal areas in the country and interacted with the cross-sections of the society besides evaluating the administration of the Scheduled Areas under the 5th Schedule of the Constitution, particularly, in regard to the functioning of the TACs, laws applicable to the Scheduled Areas and the exercises of powers by the Governors concerned under the 5th Schedule of the Constitution, principles to be followed in notifying Scheduled Areas, the welfare of Scheduled Tribes through the various development programmes directed to uplift them and any other matters connected with the administration of Scheduled Areas or the welfare of the Scheduled Tribes.

Assessment

The Commission after investigating the subjects of reference at great length found positive effects of the various plans and programmes during the 1st and the 2nd five Year Plans. The appreciable work in the field of education by opening large number of schools including Ashrams and Sevashrams and supply of text-books and scholarships, construction of roads, bridle paths and hill paths, grain banks, multipurpose societies, organised forest labour, and efforts for settled agriculture were noted by the Commission. But, the gap to be bridged between the Scheduled Areas and surrounding areas and the Scheduled Tribes and others still remained large, the Commission observed. The necessity to give priority to the development of communication network in the Scheduled Areas and promotion of education among tribals was considered most essential to break their isolation. Assimilation through development intervention along with protective measures was the sum and substance of the Commission's assessment. The Commission did not talk about the so-called self induced development of tribal people leading to self-reliance along the line of their genius without development intervention from outside, which was considered an imposition in different forms by the Expert Committee headed by Verrier Elwin. The assessment of the Tribal Development made by the Commission appears as relevant today as it was 40 years back. Some of the important recommendations are mentioned in brief as follows:

Recommendations of the Commission

Tribal Concentration in Scheduled Area

The percentage of tribal concentration in any area proposed for declaration as scheduled area should not be less than 50% for protective measures and large scale development. The compactness of area is an important consideration to declare the scheduled area since scheduling involves special administration. The sub-tehsil to be coterminus with a tribal development block should be a principal unit of administration. The area should be under-developed. There should be marked disparity in the economic standard of tribals living in areas compared to the people in the surrounding areas.

Contents of Governors Reports

Governors reports are intended to enable the Union government to discharge their responsibilities to the tribes. This purpose has not been fulfilled. The Union Government should issue instructions about the formal contents of these reports. The Governors report should be handled by Chief Secretary and should invariably go to the Council of Ministers before being forwarded to the Governor and through him to the President. The TAC should also be invited to make suggestion for inclusion in the report on any matter of importance.

There should be a special machinery in the States to consider possible efforts of legislation proposed in the Parliament and State legislature on the tribals.

Representation of TAC

Tribes Advisory Council should have staff of its own with a Secretary who can do the follow-up work. Chairman of the TAC should be a person who has influence beyond the department concerned. The representation of officials should be limited to one at the most so as to leave scope for nomination of non-officials. TAC should be in all the States whether they have scheduled areas or not to advise protection and development of Scheduled Tribes.

Development of Tribal Areas

The 5th Schedule of the Constitution is conceived as a temporary expedient and its objective can be achieved by an alternative approach, which is simply that Government should undertake a plan which would protect the Scheduled Tribes and ensure development of the tribal areas within a stated period. No scheduled area should be de-scheduled unless the Government after examination of all available data certifies that the scheduled area fulfills a certain standard and has developed economically and educationally in points of health, communications and services to the limit when it can no longer remain scheduled.

Maintenance of Development Expenditure Figures

The figures of developmental expenditure should be maintained district wise as unless the scheduled area is itself a district, it is impossible to get physical and financial targets achieved in the scheduled areas. The distribution of grants-in-aid under Article 275 of the Constitution should not be only on the basis of population. The criteria may also include level of development reached by the State in welfare activities for STs, level of administration for scheduled areas and financial position of the State. The problem of economic development can not be solved unless the resources of land, cattle-wealth, cottage industries and village industries are all mobilized with an integrated approach.

Mobilization of Education Programmes

Education has made unmistakable impact on tribal mind making more demand for it. The process of spreading education by opening schools with qualified teachers in the scheduled areas should be accelerated. Residential schools should be opened in the remote areas for tribal people. Primary education in the tribal areas should be the responsibility of the State Education Department. Tribal welfare should be separated from social welfare. Funds available under the Block Programmes for education should be administered by the education department. More funds from the general revenue for expenditure on education should be allotted bearing in mind the reality of backwardness in tribal areas. The educational session should not coincide with agricultural and forest operations and social activities in the locality. Special emphasis should be given to crafts or to a technical bias, as far as possible. The idea of residential education should be encouraged. Equipment in primary schools should be improved, continuously. Medium of instruction in the schools in the first 2 years should be in the local tribal dialect. Adequate provisions for mid-day meal, supply of uniforms and free books should be made. Teachers in tribal areas should have thorough knowledge of tribal life and culture. There should be a separate cadre for teachers serving tribal areas for a period of 20 years.

Amendment of Laws

Existing Acts and regulations affecting tribal people should be examined and amended, drastically. The Governors may in exercise of the powers under 5th schedule issue necessary regulations without delay. There should be a general prohibition on transfer of tribal land without the permission of Deputy Commissioners or Collectors. There should be a bar against suit or application against the orders made by the Deputy Commissioner regarding restoration of land to tribals. The Deputy Commissioner should have powers *suomotu* or at the instance of the aggrieved within a period of 12 years to institute inquiries and restore possession of land to tribals. In the scheduled areas, priorities should be given to tribal people for allotment of land. The scheme for rehabilitation of displaced persons in tribal areas as a result of any project should be made part of the project expenditure.

Improvement of Agricultural and Allied Activities

Settlers in the forest villages should be granted security of tenure. Improvement of agriculture for the tribals has to follow the same principles of intensive cultivation introduced in the other parts of the country. The solution of the shifting cultivation is through terraced cultivation on the hill slopes. A programme of soil conservation should be prepared for every tribal block providing for contour bunding, Galli plugging, terracing, and field bunding, etc. The demand for irrigation should be met by reviewing and revising rules in relation to returns. The question of returns should be considered in the light of the condition of tribal people. There is considerable scope for development of horticulture if technical assistance and guidance is made available. Food preservation units, storage, transport and market facilities should be provided in the scheduled areas.

Protection/Production of Village Industries

The village industries can be divided into three categories: (a) Consumer good industries (b) Processing industries and (c) Handicrafts and art pieces. Raw-materials from the tribal areas should not go in the form of raw-materials but go as processed goods, as far as possible. The skill of tribal people should be upgraded to the requirement of cottage industries by opening Training Centres.

Discharge of Debts

The creditors should be required to file their claims against the tribal debtors within a prescribed time after which the right of action should be carried and the debt should be deemed as discharged. They should be required to produce books or other proofs in support of their claims.

Establishing of Cooperative Societies

The cooperative laws should meet the needs of tribals owning land in common in the name of their headmen or otherwise. Education in cooperation should be provided to tribals in general. Every village should be served by a cooperative society with at least one member from each family as member.

Provision of Medical Facilities

Efforts should be made to train the local people in the scientific health and hygiene. Mobile medical units should be increased with a propaganda section on health education.

Careful Planning of Roads and Houses

Housing scheme should benefit those who are in real need of house. The houses need not be costly nor built with imported materials. Highest priority should be given to roads and other forms of communications which is essential for national defense, industrialisation, implementation of welfare and development projects, commercial activities and administration of other services. Government should take programme of roads to connect more villages with markets and schools. Forest and public works department roads should be planned as a coordinated system of communications with proper regard to the protection and development of forests.

Programmes for Tribal Welfare and Rehabilitation

The Scheme for rehabilitation should include programmes for education training and equipment for the displaced people. Industrial Training Institutes should be opened to increase employability of tribal families affected by the industrial projects. The scheme of compensation should include rehabilitation within the project itself.

There should be a separate department for tribal welfare in States having sizeable tribal population. Required administrative facility should be ensured by reorganising the procedure in dealing with tribal affairs. Field staff should be carefully selected and placed in separate cadres. There should be a separate Commissioner for Scheduled Tribes who should focus attention on certain items of strategic importance.

The report by Dhebar Commission was the most comprehensive exercise covering almost every aspect of tribal affairs. The assessment was realistic and recommendations pragmatic. The strategies for tribal development which were worked out during the fourth and fifth Five Year

Plans were based on the Commission's report, although it would be unrealistic to conclude that the recommendations were fully implemented. Indeed, the Expert Committees constituted during the subsequent years endorsed the findings of Dhebar Commission and pleaded for vigorous implementations of its recommendations.

Report of the Study Team on Tribal Development Programmes

A study team on tribal development programme with the object of giving practical effect to the recommendations made in the 4th 5 year plan draft for welfare of Scheduled Tribes and for assisting State Governments in evolving concrete schemes of development, especially adapted to the needs of tribal communities and scheduled areas was constituted by the Planning Commission under the Chairmanship of P. Shilu Ao in October, 1966. The Committee was asked to

(a) look into the problems and needs of tribal communities in each State;

(b) apprise the working of tribal development programmes, especially during 3rd five Year Plan;

(c) ascertain how far the schemes formulated so far have enabled the tribal communities to secure an adequate share in the benefits accruing from the general development programmes;

(d) make detailed recommendations regarding the lines on which the schemes should be oriented in the 4th Five Year Plan to accelerate progress; and

(e) suggest measures for strengthening the administrative machinery and harnessing tribal leadership to ensure their fullest participation in the task of economic and social development.

Recommendations

The Committee submitted its report in September, 1969 making a serious and realistic assessment on the prevailing State of tribal affairs and development of Scheduled Areas. The Committee pronounced boldly:

> "There are three principal groups of tribes in India. On one end of the scale we have tribes living in the fastnesses of the hills cut off from all contact with the outer world, who are still in the hunting stage, at the other end we find a virile race of freedom-loving, politically conscious tribals in North East India many of whom, through the devoted efforts of missionaries for over a century, have reached a stage when they can rub shoulders even with their most

enlightened counterparts amongst the advanced communities. And in between we see, in the vast tribal belt which stretches like a girdle across Central India from Orissa (including Andhra) in the East to Gujarat in the West, tribals in varying stages of development" (page 10-11).

The Committee (popularly known as Shilu Ao. Committee) felt it unrealistic to proceed on the basis that integration of diverse tribal communities can not be reached over a short period of time. The Committee also recommended resolute action to deschedule the more advanced tribal communities on the one hand and to exclude communities which ought never to have been included in the Scheduled Tribes (page 12). A section of communities notified under the Criminal Tribes Act, 1924 during the Colonial Administration, denotified after independence should also be included in the list of Scheduled Tribes as they possess all the characteristics of tribes and the stamp of past continues to haunt them making their assimilation with the rest of the society difficult, the Committee observed. It was emphasized that the development of tribals along the lines of their genius should not be misunderstood to make the tribes more picturesque anthropological specimens to be retained as subjects of study by social anthropologists. The tribals have to be assisted to progress both economically and socially to reach standards of development which would allow them on the footing of equality *vis-à-vis* the general community. The main recommendations made by the Committee are as follows:

Tribal Development Programmes

Vigorous efforts should be made to implement the recommendations made by the Sheduled Areas and Scheduled Tribes Commission and other high level bodies in the past to protect the rights of tribals and implement tribal development programmes.

Conscious attempts should be made to ensure that tribals received a reasonable share of the benefits from the general development programmes. Planning Commission should stipulate as a condition of approval of the State plans that the general development programmes should take into consideration the needs of tribals and indicate the directions. The extent to which the general programmes are expected to benefit the tribal communities should not only be indicated in the State plans but should also be monitored by a permanent Cell to be established in the evaluation wing of the Planning Commission.

Special Provisions for Development of Backward Areas

A reasonable percentage of the special provisions made by the Planning Commission should be earmarked specifically for the development of more backward areas amongst the tribal regions. The tribal development programmes should be exhibited separately and not as a part of the social services. As recommended by the Scheduled Areas and Scheduled Tribes Commission, non-lapsable Tribal Welfare Fund should be constituted. In the implementation of schemes, steps should be taken to anticipate and avoid mistakes which lead to the failure of land colonization schemes. Social and economic advancement of tribals lies in the judicious synthesis of the T. D. Block and area development approach.

Land Settlement and Restoration

Survey and settlement of tribal areas should be completed expeditiously so that pattas are granted to the tribals on the land being cultivated by them which would improve their economic condition and creditworthiness. The Governors should exercise their powers under the 5th schedule of the Constitution to ensure restoration of tribal land transferred to the non-tribals and other necessary protective measures.

Educational Facilities

Central schools and residential schools should be established in remote tribal areas at selected centres with facilities for the teaching of science and mathematics by well paid capable teachers. Education being a key and critical input for overall development, schools should be opened to cover each tribal village by the State Education Department. Primary schools should be opened within one or two miles of the home of every child thus relaxing the normal norms. In sparsely populated areas, Ashram Schools should be established. Teachers should be given attendance allowance on the basis of enrolment and attendance of tribal children. All tribal children should be given free books, writing materials, clothes and Mid-day Meals. School hours should be fixed to suit the work the children are required to do to assist their families.

Reclamation of Land and Agricultural Improvement

Where sizeable tracts of land are available, mechanized reclamation should be undertaken at Government Cost and developed land allotted to the tribals. Efforts should be made to regulate the shifting cultivation along scientific lines and wean away the tribals from this practice systematically. Steps should be taken to make subsistence oriented tribal agriculture more remunerative with improved methods like distribution of suitable agricultural implements, demonstration farms and credit facilities. The procedure for disposal of applications for granting loans by Cooperative Societies should be demystified and simplified in respect of tribals. Minor irrigation projects should be executed expeditiously in the tribal areas along with development of marketing infrastructure.

Forest Rights to Tribals

Tribals should be given privileges and concessions in the forest areas considering the symbiotic relationship without a legalistic approach in regard to their forest right.

Establishment of Forest Welfare Developments

Control of Tribal Blocks should vest in the Tribal Welfare Department which has an intimate knowledge about the tribal areas and needs of tribal people. The budget of TD blocks should be sufficiently flexible to enable the schemes to be reoriented to suit the felt needs of tribal people.

Medical Facilities

Primary health centres should be located in places where they can cater to the needs of as many villages as possible. Health education should spread among the tribals through audio-vidual methods. More emphasis should be given to the preventive measures and more mobile dispensaries should be started. Beds should be reserved for tribal patients in general leprosy hospitals and steps should be taken to organise leprosy surveys through qualified doctors.

Careful Planning of Roads

In programme of road construction, special attention should be paid to the needs of tribal areas. Long roads should be constructed to connect valleys with the main road. Priority should be given to such roads as can be used throughout the year and those which link up the tribal villages with the weekly markets, hospitals, dispensaries and schools. Rail links should be extended to the tribal areas to the maximum.

Administration and Welfare of Tribes

Administration in the tribal areas should be effective and geared to suit the requirement of a population living in widely sundered and often inaccessible places and should take into account the primitive nature of existence. The tribal welfare should not be clubbed with the welfare of Scheduled Castes and other backward classes. Separate district officers for tribal welfare should be appointed to work under the Director, Tribal Welfare at the State level. Posting of officers in areas having considerable tribal population should be done on selective basis. To make the service conditions attractive, special allowances and incentives should be given to those serving in the tribal areas. The administrative machinery at the district and at the State level should be organised on lines suggested by the Scheduled Area and Scheduled Tribe Commission.

The report of Shilu Ao Committee was a pragmatic assessment of achievement and desired course of action during the Fourth Five Year Plan for betterment. It called for a long term, realistic and comprehensive programmes with higher allocations under the general and specific sectors of scheme to develop the tribal communities who stood at different levels of development across the country. In substance, the report pleaded for implementation of Dhebar Commission Report.

Report of the Committee of Members of Parliament and Experts Constituted to Make Recommendations on Law Concerning Extension of Provisions of the Constitution (Seventy-third Amendment) Act, 1992 to Scheduled Areas (Bhuria Committee Report)

The Ministry of Rural Development, Government of India constituted a Committee comprising Tribal Members of Parliament and Experts under the chairmanship of Sri Dileep Singh Bhuria in July, 1994 to make recommendations for extending provisions of the 73rd Constitution Amendment Act, 1992 to Scheduled Areas. The Committee (known as Bhuria Committee) submitted its report in January, 1995 after assessing the existing state of Panchayat Raj Institutions in the Scheduled Areas and recommended extension of Panchayat provisions to Scheduled Areas with certain modifications keeping in view the special provisions for administration of these areas under 5th and 6th Schedule of the Constitution. The Constitution Act, 1992 devolved on Panchayats powers and authority to enable them to function as Institutions of Self-Governance with respect to preparation and implementation of plans for economic development and social justice but did not take into account the unique features of tribal areas.

Observations

The Committee observed that the provisions of the Constitution Amendment Act, 1992 could not apply automatically to the scheduled and tribal areas as they do not go hand in hand with the constitutional scheme for governing these areas under the 5th and 6th Schedule of the Constitution. The 5th Schedule provides for tribal consultative machinery in form of a 'Tribes Advisory Council' and a paternalistic design to prevent tribal communities from being exploited. Under this Schedule, Governors of States having Scheduled Areas are vested with powers to issue Regulations having the same force as of law and adapting laws passed by

Parliament and State Legislatures to protect the tribal interests. The Central Government not only have a constitutional obligation to provide Grant in Aid from the Consolidated Fund of India for socio-economic development and raising the level of administration in the Scheduled Areas, but is also empowered to issue directions for governing these areas. The 6th Schedule promotes the concept of self-management for Autonomous Councils and Regional Councils at the district and regional levels, respectively, with no provisions for democratic or traditional organisations below the district level.

Recommendations

The Committee observed that the extension of Panchayats to the Scheduled Areas should be in harmony with the traditional structures, practices and customary laws. The new structures should have enough powers for combating and preventing exploitation of tribal communities in addition to dealing with the problem of indebtedness, deforestation, ecology degradation on account of industrialization and excise policy, etc, without disturbing the traditional arrangements. The main recommendations made by the Committee are as follows:

Recognition of the Gram Sabha and Gram Panchayat

The traditional system of Gram Sabha which is the main decision-making body through consensus should be recognised respecting the customary codes, at the village or hamlet level. The autonomy of this most important grass-root body should not be interfered with through any manipulation. The Gram Sabha may have its own executive Council. The next level should be that of Gram Panchayat to be composed of elected representatives from a group of villages or hamlets.

Recognition of the Taluka Panchayat

The next level of the Panchayat may be called by the name Taluka Panchayat or Panchayat Samity, etc. This intermediate level Panchayat should be coterminus with a Development Block. The MLAs and MPs belonging to tribal communities should be allowed to be members of this intermediate level Panchayat.

Recognition of Autonomous District Council

The third tier of Panchayat at the district level should be called Autonomous District Council as envisaged under the 6th Schedule of the Constitution. As at the intermediate level, the MLAs and MPs belonging to tribal communities should be made members of this district level Council. The Autonomous Council should have legislative, judicial, executive and financial powers concerning allotment, occupation and use of land; management of forest, management of minor forest produce; management of water resources; regulations of practice of shifting cultivation; establishment of town Committees or councils and their powers; matters relating to villages or town administration including villages or town police, appointment or succession of chief, customary laws including inheritance, marriage, divorce, etc., local customs, control of money lending and trading by non-tribals, excise and laws regarding partnership of local communities in enterprise based on local resources.

PRIs to Decide on Policy Issues.....

The Panchayat Raj Institutions of scheduled areas and tribal areas should have access and command over natural resources with a view to utilising them for sustainable development. In the name of democracy, the unified policy of tribal community should not be divided on the party lines. The Constitution Amendment Acts promoting local self governance in rural and urban areas should be interpreted and interlinked with the provisions of the 5th and 6th Schedule and nothing inconsistent with each other should be viewed between these two Schedules. Some changes in the overall design of 6th Schedule could serve as a frame within the power canvas of the 5th Schedule.

Within a period of two years, States should think of reorganizing the existing administrative boundaries based on ethnic, demographic and geographic considerations for a rational delimitation. Since the Scheduled Areas are expected to have majority of tribal population, majority of seats in Panchayats at all levels should be reserved for them even if in a few Scheduled Areas, the demographic composition has changed in favour of non-tribals. The Chairperson and Vice-Chairperson in Panchayats at all levels should belong to STs and 1/3rd of the seats should be reserved for women.

The Panchayats in the Scheduled Areas should be paid Grant in Aid under Article 275 (1) of the Constitution for scheme of tribal development and administration of scheduled areas without debarring them from receiving other funds like under Article 243(h) and 243(I). Management and utilization of financial resources assigned to Panchayats should be within competence of these bodies. Funds should be received by the District Council directly from the Central and State Governments and distributed among the lower tier Panchayats.

As evident, the exercise done by Bhuria Committee is to facilitate extension of Panchayat Provisions to the Scheduled Areas to implement the 73rd constitutional amendment, without tampering with the traditional decision-making structures which have greater force and effectiveness among the tribal communities. The Committee has made attempts to harmonize between the conflicting provisions of 5th and 6th Schedule on the one hand and the Constitution Act, 1992, on the other. However, the excessive stress on the 5th and 6th Schedules of the Constitution which were expected to be transitory provisions to integrate the tribal sections of our society with the rest of the population without being exploited, appears to be in conflict with the present day realities. The Committee has ignored the fact that all the Development Blocks in the Scheduled Areas did not have majority of tribal population at any point of time. In deed, the inaccessable areas notified as 'excluded' and 'partially excluded' by the Colonial Administration were specified as Scheduled Areas in the Constitution Order, 1950. The same position was reiterated in 1977, although Dhebar Commission had clearly recommended to notify Blocks under the Scheduled Area if above 50 per cent of the population comprised tribals. There are many Blocks (for example Rajmahal, Sahibhanj and Barharva in Sahebhanj district and Dhalmum in East Sinhabhum district of Jharkhand State) with less then 12 per cent tribal population in Scheduled Areas. Reservation of majority of seats and chairpersionship of Panchayats at all levels in such Blocks for tribals would create conflicts with other sections of the society besides failing to withstand the test of judicial scrutiny. In fact, this recommendation of Bhuria Committee on being reflected in the Panchayat Provisions (Extension to Scheduled Area) Act, 1996 has already created an anomalous situation leading to litigation and Social Conflicts.

4

Tribal Scene in Orissa

Tribes in Orissa

There are as many as 62 communities, which have been recognised as Scheduled Tribes in Orissa under Article 342 of the Constitution. Section 4 of the Constitution (Scheduled Tribes) Order 1950 as amended in 1976 notifies the following communities as the Scheduled Tribes:

1. Bagata, 2. Baiga, 3. Banjara, Banjari, 4. Bathudi, 5. Bhattoda, Dhotada, 6. Bhuiya, Bhuyan, 7. Bhumia, 8. Bhumij, 9. Bhunijia, 10. Binjhal, 11. Binjhia, Binjhoa, 12. Birhor, 13. Bondo Poraja, 14. Chenchu, 15. Dal, 16. Desua Bhumij, 17. Dharua, 18. Didayi, 19. Gadaba, 20. Gandia, 21. Ghara, 22. Gond, Gondo, 23. Ho, 24. Holva, 25. Jatapu, 26. Juang, 27. Kandha Gauda, 28. Kawar, 29. Kharia, Kharian, 30. Kharwar, 31. Khond, Kond, Kandha, Nanguli Kandh, Sitha Kandha, 32. Kisan, 33. Kol, 34. Kolah Loharas, Kol Loharas, 35. Kolha, 36. Koli, Malhar, 37. Kondadora, 38. Kora, 39. Korua, 40. Kotia, 41. Koya, 42. Kolis, 43. Lodha, 44. Madia, 45. Mahali, 46. Mankidi, 47. Mankirdia, 48. Matya, 49. Mirdhas, 50. Munda, Munda Lohara, Munda Mahalis, 51. Mundari, 52. Omanatya, 53. Oraon, 54. Parenga, 55. Paroja, 56. Pentia, 57. Rajuar, 58. Santal, 59. Saora, Savar, Saira. Sahara, 60. Shabar, Lodha, 61. Sounti, 62. Tharua.

The total tribal population in the State of Orissa was 70.32 lakhs which worked out to be 22.16 per cent of the total population, according to 1991 Census. The growth in the Tribal population is lower than that of others is evident from the fact that the percentage of tribals to the total population which was 22.39 per cent according to 1981 Census in the State got reduced to 22.16 per cent in 1991. The females (33.45 lakhs) outnumber the males (33.25 lakhs) and except a small portion of their population, which resides in urban areas (3.62 lakhs), they still live in the rural areas and in relative isolation. The ten less known tribal communities with population below 2000 each in the State are Baiga (1556), Birhor (825), Chenchu (275), Desua : Bhumij (1880), Ghara (1553), Korua (1989), Madia (1439), Mankidi (1150), Mankirdia 1491) and Tharua (1595). While there are a few tribal communities with their presence in certain specified areas, the communities having larger population have their presence in almost all the districts where tribals are either in majority or have significant presence. The tribe wise distribution of tribal population in different (undivided) districts of Orissa according to 1991 Census is indicated in Annexures I to XIII. Some of the important features are mentioned in beief as below:

1. Bagata

Bagatas are one of the lesser known tribes in Orissa with a total population of 4806, according to 1991 census. Despite being a small group, they are found all over the State. More than 50 Per cent of their population however, resides in Sundargarh and Koraput districts. Bagatas have adjusted themselves to the local environmental situation and changing socio-economic conditions. In coastal areas, catching fish in fresh water has become an occupation for them. But, they still depend upon shifting cultivation for survival in Kotpad area of Nawarangpur. There are two main sections of Bagata tribe, namely, Vaishnavites and Shaivites.

2. Baiga

Baigas are a very small tribe in Orissa with a population of 1556, as per 1991 census. They are mostly found in Sundargarh and Nawarangpur districts. Baigas are broadly divided into seven groups namely, Binjhwar, Bharotia, Narotia or Nahar, Raibhaine, Kathabhaina, Kondwan or Kundi and Gondwaine. The Baigas appear to be a branch of the Bhumia tribe. They claim to be superior to the Gonds. Agriculture and minor forest produce are the principal means of their livelihood. Baigas are very religious. The deities worshiped by them are Bara Deo, Thakur Deo, Dhariti Mata, Bhimasen, Ganesh Deo. They regard themselves as the most powerful magicians in the world.

3. Banjara

Banjaras are one of the little known tribes of Orissa. Their total population in the State is 12,843 as per 1991 census. They are mainly found in the districts of Kalahandi, Koraput and Sambalpur. The process of modernization has transformed on their traditional life. The principal sources of their livelihood include agriculture, minor forest produce and wage earnings.

4. Bathudi

Major concentration of this community is found in Karanjia and Kaptipada sub-divisions of Mayurbhanj district, Champua and Keonjhar sub-divisions of Keonjhar district and Nilgiri sub-division of Balasore district. The total population belonging to this community in Orissa according to 1991 census is 1.71 lakhs. The main economic activity of Bathudis is settled agriculture. Their socio-economic practices are similar to their other Hindu neighbours. They claim to be descendents of sages like Parasar, Nageswar, Sailya, Ganeswar, Kashyap, Dhandpula, Bhardwaj, etc. Brahmin priests are invited by them to perform rituals like Shradha. They workship the same Hindu deities and celebrate the same Festivals like the Hindus.

5. Bhottoda

Bhattodas are famous for efficiency in improved agricultural practices. According to some Anthropologists, Bhattodas constitute a sub-division of Gond tribe of Bastar. They have sizeable presence in Nawarangpur and Koksara and Jaipatna Blocks of Kalahandi district. Their presence in other districts is small and sporadic. According to 1991 census, the population of this community in Orissa is 3.04 lakhs with males (1.36 lakhs) being comprehensively outnumbered by females (1.68 lakhs). They have been fully integrated with Hindus for which their tribal origin has been questioned by some scholars. They speak Oriya language and perform festivals and rituals in the same manner as their Hindu neighbours. They also believe in re-birth.

6. Bhuyan

This is one of the primitive tribes in the State with it's concentration in Banspal Block of Kaonjhar district. The total population of Bhuyan tribe according to 1991 census is 2.47 lakhs with females (1.25 lakhs) outnumbering marginally their male counterparts (1.22 lakhs). Shifting cultivation alongwith collection of minor forest produce is the primary source of sustenance for a large section of Bhuyan people. However, they are also moving fast towards settled cultivation, fishing, wage earning, trading, industrial employment etc. One of the sections of this tribe called 'Poudi Bhuyan' has been identified as a' primitive tribe' in Orissa. The two major deities worshiped by Bhyana people are known as Dharam Devata (Sun God) and Basuki Mata (Earth Goddess). The head of the main village is called Sardar, a powerful post traditionally.

7. Bhumia

The major section of Bhumias inhabit Nawarangpur (formerly Koraput) district. Their presence in Sambalpur, Boudh-Khandmal, Ganjam-Gajapati and Sundargarh districts is sporadic and scattered. The population of Bhumias according to 1991 census is 1.10 lakhs. They are settled agriculturists with rice being supplemented by millets, pulses, vegetables, tubers, etc. as their main staple food. The impact of modernization is perceptible in their social life.

8. Bhumij

Bhumijs are found mainly in Mayurbhanj district. According to some Anthropologists, they are a branch of Munda tribe, greatly influenced by socio-cultural practices of their Hindu neighbours. Their population according to 1991 census is 1.78 lakhs. They are settled agriculturists. The urge for upward mobility among the Bhumijs can be guessed from the fact that they work in large number as industrial workers and in tea gardens of the north-east India.

9. Bhunjia

Numerically, this is a small tribe with a population of 11,276 according to 1991 census. Described to be of Dravidian racial group, Bhunjias have been divided into two sections, namely, Chukuti Bhunjia and Chinda Bhunjia. The former with its concentration in a specified pockets bordering Madhya Paadesh is identified as a 'primitive tribe' for micro level socio-economic rehabilitation. They mainly reside in Nuapada (formerly Kalahandi) district. Almost fully integrated with Hindu social structure, Bhunjias communicate in a dialect forming part of Hindi family. Rice is their main staple food and agriculture the, primary source of subsistence. Shifting cultivation is still being practised by them, sporadically.

10. Binjhal

Although linguistically Binjhals are considered to belong to Dravidian group, they speak Oriya language, by and large. Their main concentration is in Sambalpur and Bolangir districts. They are stated to have come to Orissa from Central India. The population of Binjhals according to 1991 census is 1.20 lakhs. Their main economic activity is settled agriculture. Like their non-tribal counterparts, they grow paddy, pulses and a number of vegetables. Having adopted Hindu Gods, Goddess, and festivals, they have assimilated into the social mainstream.

11. Binjhia

Binjhias are spread over Bihar (now in Jharkhand), West Bengal, Orissa and Madhya Pradesh. Majority of them reside in Sundergarh, Bolangir, Kheonjhar districts. They believe to be the descendents of Goddess Vindhyavasini who migrated to Orissa from the Vindhya Valley of Central India. The total population of Binjhials according to 1991 census is 8,128. The socio-cultural practices followed by the community are similar to those of local Hindus. Rituals like marriage and Shradha are performed according to Hindu customs. They claim to be on par with Hindu Rajputs.

12. Birhor

Birhors belong to the category of hunting and gathering groups. They wander from place to place and are known as a nomadic tribe. Their population, according to 1991 census in Orissa is only 825. They are known as Mankidi in Kalahandi and Sundergarh districts and Mankirdia in Sambalpur and Mayurbhanj. As the names suggest, they are employed in rural areas for catching monkeys who play havoc in damaging crops, fruits and vegetables. They live in places close to the forests which is also their main source of subsistence. A micro project has been set up for the socio-economic rehabilitation of Birhors, who have been identified as a 'primitive tribe' in the State.

13. Bondo

Once regarded as criminals among the tribes, Bondos inhabit hilly regions of Malkangiri (formerly Koraput) on the north-west Muchkund river. The total population of Bondo tribe is 7,315 according to 1990-91 census. Their language called Remo comes under Mundari group of the Astro-Asiatic language. Bondos are divided into three sub-groups, namely: upper hill group, foot hill group and plain area group. Those forming part of the first group are known for their instinctive and aggressive behaviour and social isolation. They move with bows and arrows and turn violent with a slight provocation. Being identified as a 'primitive tribe', a micro project has been set up for implementing schemes for their socio-economic rehabilitation. Agriculture their chief source of livelihood is being adopted by them gradually.

14. Chenchu

Chenchus are the smallest tribe in Orissa. According to the 1991 census their population is 275 only. They are known as a South Indian Tribe and found in certain parts of Koraput and Gajapati districts bordering Andhra Pradesh.

15. Dal

This is a small tribe with a population of 9,867 according to 1991 census. They are found in southern and western parts of Bolangir and Kalahandi districts. People belonging to this tribe follow socio-economic practices and cultural rituals of their Hindu neighbours. Agriculture is the principal source of their livelihood and hunting and collection of minor forest produce are part time activities. Having assimilated with the social mainstream, they observe festivals and rituals according to the Hindu calendar year.

16. Desia Bhumij

Desia Bhumijs are a section of the Bhumija Tribe of Orissa. Their population according to 1991 census is 1880. They are mostly found in Mayurbhanj district. They consider themselves to be superior to the Bhumija Tribe, who live in the same areas. Agriculture is the principal source of their subsistence. The income derived from agriculture is supplemented by the minor forest produce and wage earnings.

17. Dharua

This is one of the oldest tribes of Orissa found in most districts. Dharuas are divided into different clans like Soma, Surya, Yadu, Kadamb, Gangu, Garg, etc., and are known as Kshatriya stocks. They observe most of Hindu rituals and, festivals besides worshiping Gods and Goddesses. Dharuas are one of the most advanced tribes in the State. Their population according to 1991 census is 11,512. Majority of them live in Koraput and Mayurbhanj districts. Traditionally, agriculture is their main occupation. They used to be employed by local rulers for military services.

18. Didayi

This tribe constitutes a small group confined to hill ranges of eastern ghat in Malkangiri district. Elwin Varrier has described Didayis as a wild tribe. According to local lores, Bondos were their elder brothers and other tribes like Godaba and Paroja were also from their community. The economy of Didayis is subsistence oriented with shifting cultivation still being in practice. Collection of minor forest produce, hunting, domestication of wild animals, and wage earning are the other economic activities for supplementing the family income. The community is well organised in specified territories. Being notified as a 'primitive tribe' a micro project has been set up for its socio-economic rehabilitation. According to 1991 census, Didayi population is 5471.

19. Gadaba

This is an old and colourful tribe of Orissa which mainly inhabits southern part of Koraput district. Gadaba population according to 1991 census is 67,138. according to the local legends the original home of Gadabas is the Vindhya Mountains. Their economy is agriculture based, which is supplemented by minor forest produce, hunting, fishing and wage earning. Shifting cultivation on hill slopes has almost been abandoned by the community. Minor millets, ragi and nizer are the main crops grown by Gadabas on the undulated land. Plain land is utilized for growing paddy drawing water from the perennial and semi-perennial hill streams. Horticultural crops like mangoes and jack-fruits are grown by them, extensively. Gadabas use cattle for plough and not milk. The community is divided into five main sections : Bada Gadaba, Parenga Gadaba, Sana Gadaba, Ollar Gadaba and Kapu Gadaba. The total Gadaba population according to 1991 census is 67,138.

20. Gandia

Gandias are a section of Koya Tribe. The Koyas treat Gandias as inferior to them. According to a local lore, they were driven out by Koyas from their community having come to know about their habits of stealing cattle. Those ostracized formed a separate community called Gandia. Gandias largely depend upon forests and wage earnings for their survival. Their lifestyle and culture is the same as Koyas. The population of Gandia tribe is 3588 (1991 census); the male female ratio being almost equal.

21. Ghara

The population of Gharas in the State according to 1991 census is 1553 with the sex ratio in favour of the females. They are mostly found in Sambalpur, Bolangir and adjoining areas. Gharas are regarded as a section of the Gond Tribe. They depend on agriculture and wage earnings for their survival.

22. Gond

This most predominant tribal community of India has sizeable presence in Orissa. According to 1991 census, the population of Gonds in the State is 7.01 lakhs. They are divided into two groups in the State. Those living in Sundargarh, Balasore, Sambalpur and parts of Kalahandi are highly acculturated under the influence of Hindu custom. They hire services of Brahmin priests for performing religious rituals and claim status of warrior caste called Kshatriya. They speak Oriya language. Others living in Koraput and other parts of Kalahandi district have retained their distinctiveness in terms of dress, habits and cultural practices. They speak Gondi, which belongs to Dravidian family.

23. Ho

This community is known by the popular epithet 'kol'. However, Hos dislike to be addressed as 'Kol' which means 'boar' in Sanskrit. They do not inhabit any specific compact area and live mostly in scattered villages having mixed population, throughout the State. According to 1991 census, their population is 50,892 with the sex ratio in favour of the females. Hos admit having descended from the common family of Mundas and claim to have their origin in Chota Nagpur area from where they migrated to Mayurbhanj and Khonjhar districts. They are settled agriculturists and their food habits are the same as others in the villages they live. Apart from agriculture, they also collect minor forest produce and work as industrial workers in mining areas. They have adopted some of the festivals and rituals of the Hindu calendar. Brahmin Priests are called by them for performing marriages and other important religious rites.

24. Holva

The nama Holva seems to be derivative of 'Hola' meaning 'plough'. People forming part of this community inhabit southern districts of Koraput and Kalahandi bordering Andhra Pradesh. Their presence in Sundergarh, Kheojhar, Sambalpur and other districts is sporadic. According to 1991 census, population of Holvas is 30,662 with the sex ratio favouring the females. They worship a number of Hindu Gods/ Goddess like Shiva, Vishnu, Laxmi, Kali, Durga, etc, and observe many Hindu rituals. Their dress and food habits are the same as their Hindu neighbours. Dead bodies are cremated except those of women who die during the pregnancy. Agriculture is the main source of their livelihood.

25. Jatapu

The Madras census report of 1901 describes Jatapus as a civilized section of Kondhs, who consider themselves to be superior (to Kondhs). They are mainly found in Koraput and Ganjam/Gajpati districts. Their population according to 1991 census is 9,139. The primary occupation of Jatapus is agriculture. They do not practise shifting cultivation. Rice and Ragi constitute their staple food. The income derived from agriculture is supplemented by minor forest produce. Pongal and Pondugu are among the major festivals observed by them.

26. Juang

Juangs are found in hill ranges of Keonjhar and adjoining areas (Pallahada Block) of Anugul district. They do not have presence elsewhere in the country. Hill Juangs are considered more primitive than those living in the plain areas. They practise shifting cultivation. Being notified as a 'primitive tribe' in the State, a micro-project has been set up for their special economic rehabilitation. Ethnically, they are considered as a branch of Mundari group. According to a popular folklore, Juangs consider themselves to be the first human being born on earth. Rishi Tanger, a hillock near Gonasika in Keonjhar district was the original home of their ancestor Rishis. Dance and music form an integral part of their social and religious festivals. They worship Gods and Goddesses of Hindu pantheon like Shiva, Parvati, Jagannath, etc., and observe festivals like Rath Yatra, Raja Sankranti, Ganesh and Laxmi Puja, etc. Agriculture including shifting cultivation is their main economic activity for livelihood. The population of Juangs according to 1991 census is 35,665 with the females outnumbering the males.

27. Kandha Gouda

Kandha Goudas are mostly found in Kalahandi, Nayagarh and adjoining Khandmal areas. They basically belong to the Kandha tribe. Some of the Anthropologists have treated them as cross-breed of Kandha and Goudas. The traditional source of subsistence of Kandh Goudas is grazing of cattle, which is being replaced progressively by agriculture. The total population of Kandh Gouda according to 1991 census is 19,278.

28. Kawar

Kawars claim to be descendents of Kauravas of *Mahabharat* a fame. They are distributed in almost all districts with higher concentration in Sundargarh, Sambalpur and Kalahandi districts. They speak Chhattisgari dialect. The population of Kawars according to 1991 census is 9,582. Military service was considered as their traditional occupation, once upon a time. They now depend on agriculture and wage earning for their livelihood.

29. Kharia

Kharias claim to be the elder branch of Munda tribe. They are divided into three social groups, namely, Paharia Kharia (Hill Kharia), Delki Kharia, (Early comers) and Dudh Kharia (Pure Kharia). The Hill Kharias are more backward section of the tribe who still depend upon hunting, food gathering and shifting cultivation. Simlipal Hill ranges are hearth and home of Hill Kharias. Being identified as a 'primitive tribe' a micro project has been set up for their economic rehabilitation in the State. Delkis are settled cultivators and Dhudh Kharias are the most advanced ones. They live mostly in Sundargarh, Mayurbhanj and Sambalpur districts. The population of Kharias in the State according to 1991 census is 1.68 lakhs with sex ratio favouring the females.

30. Kharwar

Kharwars are mostly found in Sundargarh and Keonjhar districts. Their population in Orissa as per 1991 census is 3280 with the females outnumbering the males. This little known tribe subsists on agriculture and wage earning for its survival. The socio-economic life of Kharwars has been influenced due to industrialization in their area. They are struggling to adjust to changing socio-economic environments around them while preserving their traditional lifestyle and culture.

31. Kandha

Numerically, Kandha tribe forms the largest group of tribes in the State with a population of 11.40 lakhs according to 1991 census. This constitutes about 16.5 per cent of the total tribal population in Orissa. Kandhas mainly inhabit the Central and Rayagada sections of the Eastern Ghat region. Their presence in other parts of the State is sporadic. There are three main sub-groups forming part of Kandha group of tribe i.e. Dongaria Kandha, Kutia Kandha and Desia Kandha. Dongaria Kandhs inhabit Niyamgiri hills of Rayagada district (formerly Koraput) and are famous for growing fruit trees. Kutia Kandhs inhabit Belghar hills of Khandmal in Phulbani district. Both these sub groups have been identified as 'primitive tribes' in the State. Two micro projects have been formed for their economic rehabilitation. Shifting cultivation is a part and parcel of their economic life. Desia Kandhs are settled agriculturists, who represent the Hinduised Section of the tribe. The other sub groups belonging to the Kandha tribe are Malwa Kandha and Penga Kandhs whose level of development is in between shifting and settled cultivators. Kandhs are broadly divided into two linguistic groups i.e. Kui and Kuvi. The land holding pattern among the primitive sections of Kandhs is clan based which means territories are earmarked for specific clans. All the members of a clan share the land, equally. The land is not recorded in favour of anybody.

32. Kisan

Kisans form nearly 5 per cent of the total tribal population in the State. According to 1991 census, their population is 2.66 lakhs with majority of them living in Sundargarh and Sambalpur districts. People belonging to the community are efficient earth workers. They are settled agriculturists. The language and cultural traits of Kisan and Oraon tribes are similar. Dress, ornaments and other household articles used by them are similar to those of Hindus or the other tribal groups like Oraon and Gond. Their social customs include worshiping traditional Gods and Goddesses and observing religious rights connected with agricultural operations. They also celebrate festivals of Dushehra, Kali-pooja, Holi, etc. along with their Hindu neighbours. Kisans are highly assertive and conscious of their socio-economic status.

33-34. Kol, Kol Lohara

Although Kol and Kol Loharas are classified separately, they belong to the same tribal group. The political organisations, economic activities and socio-cultural functions of these groups are similar to those of Kolhas. Their population according to 1991 census is 18,098 (Kol- 2887 and Kol Loharas - 12,321) with the females outnumbering the males.

35. Kolha

Kolhas constitute one of the largest sections of tribes in Orissa. According to 1991 census, their population is 4.05 lakhs with the sex ratio in favour of the females. Some Anthropologists suggest that they are of common ancestral stock with Mundas. They mainly inhabit Mayurbhanj and Kaonjhar districts with a limited presence elsewhere. Traditionally, they subsisted on hunting but with the passage of time, they have become settled cultivators. Kolhas have been integrated with the social mainstream. They celebrate festivals and customs according to the Hindu Calendar year. The influence of Vaishnavite sect of Hinduism is noticeable in their social festivities. The decisions taken by village Panchayats having Hindu members in majority are willingly accepted by them.

36. Koli, Malhar

Although Kolis and Malhars are spread over several regions, their concentration is in Ganjam and Gajapati districts bordering Andhra Pradesh. They consider themselves above other tribal communities in the social hierarchy. Like caste Hindus, they have free access to temples and village wells. They speak Oriya and Telugu and hire Brahmin priests for religious ceremonies. Marriages are performed according to Hindu customs. Preference is given to cross-cousin marriage. Weaving is their main occupation.

Malhars are semi-nomadic. They are found in Dhenkanal-Anugul district. They earn livelihood by collecting minor forest produce and working as labour. Festivals of Hindu calendar are observed by them besides worshiping deities like Durga, Kalika, Mangla, Gramdevi, etc. The population of Kolis and Malhars according to 1991 census is 4903 with the females (2701) out numbering the males (2392).

37. Kondadora

This tribe has its presence in most districts but their main concentration is in Koraput and pockets of Kalahandi, Ganjam and Gajapati districts. One section of the tribe speaks Oriya and the other Telugu. Agriculture including shifting cultivation is the main economic activity of Kondadoras. The impact of industrialization on this community is visible as people belonging to this tribe are found working as urban and industrial workers. Their population according to 1991 census is 9,235.

38. Kora

Koras are mostly found in Dhenkanal, Angul and Sambalpur districts. They claim to be Suryavanshi Kshatriyas and observe social festivals and cultural rituals like Hindus. They consider themselves to be Saktas and Vaishnavas. Koras are rated as efficient agriculturists. They do not have a separate language or dialect. Their population according to 1991 census is 10,313.

39. Korua

Koruas are mostly found in bordering areas of Sundargarh district adjacent to Bihar. The total Korua population according to 1991 census is 1989 with females accounting for the majority. Koruas depend on forests for their survival. Most of their relatives inhabit Chhota Nagpur regions of the new State of Jharkhand.

40. Kotia

Kotias mainly live in specific areas of erstwhile districts of Koraput, Kalahandi and Phulbani. The joint family system is a common feature that differentiates this tribe from others. Their population according to 1991 census is 28,607. Kotias are agriculturists. Those not having agricultural land earn wages as agriculture labour. Pisciculture is their subsidiary occupation. The social customs of Kotias include use of sacred thread at the time of marriage. In addition to worshiping their most important deity called 'Mauli Debata' they worship Hindu Gods and Goddesses. The population of Kotias according to 1991 census is 28,607.

41. Koya

Koyas mainly inhabit Malkangiri district (formerly Koraput district) with limited presence in other parts of southern Orissa. Their population according to 1991 census is 1.42 lakhs. Though culturally a homogeneous group, they can be divided into two sub-groups. Those living in north of the district headquarter are more primitive than those on the south adjoining Andhra Pradesh. The southern Koyas are more influenced by Telugu culture. The language/dialect spoken by Koyas belongs to Dravidian group. Although Koyas have their own traditional deities and religious rituals, a number of Gods, Goddesses and festivals of Hindu pantheon have been adopted by them. They are known for their hunting and fishing skills. They seldom use cow as a milch animal. Shifting cultivation has almost been abandoned by them in favour of settled agriculture. Collection of roots, fruits, and other minor forest produce remains another means of their livelihood.

42. Kulis

Kulis are found mainly in Balangir and Padampur sub-division of Baragarh district. Their assimilation into the Hindu social structure is evident from the fact that they do not suffer from the stigma of discrimination in form. Brahming priests serve them willingly in conducting religious functions, marriage ceremonies, etc. Their primary occupation is weaving which is supplemented by agriculture. Socio-cultural practices followed by them are similar to those of Hindus. They enjoy the highest literacy rate (about 40%) among the tribals. The population of Kulis according to 1991 census is 6,526 with the sex ratio favouring the females.

43. Lodha

Lodhas suffer from the ignominy of being branded as an ex-criminal tribe. They live in villages of Mayurbhanj district adjoining Bihar and West Bengal. Lodhas trace their desceant from the famous Savaras mentioned in Hindu epics and mythology. Traditionally, they lived in jungles subsisting on hunting and food gathering. They still live in the viscinity of forests. Though, originally known to be Mundari speaking, they now speak a dialect which is a mixture of Bengali, Oriya and Mundari. Lodhas live in small villages exclusively belonging to them. They don't attach stigma to any kind of occupation. Because of instinctive and aggressive behaviours, their relationship with neighbouring communities is far from cordial. They may turn violent with a slight provocation from non-Lodhas. Lodhas believe in unseen supernatural world and observe death rituals following Hindu traditions. The total population of Lodhas in Orissa according to 1991 census is 7,458 with sex ratio in favour of the females. They have been notified as a 'primitive tribe' in the State for special economic rehabilitation through a Micro Project.

44. Madia

Madias are one of the little known tribes in Orissa. They are considered as a section of the Koya tribe. Their population according to 1991 census is 1439 with the females outnumbering their male counterparts. They are mostly found in the Balasore and Malkangiri areas. Madias depend on agriculture for their survival. Minor forest produce is the supplementary source of their subsistence.

45-46. Mankidi, Mankirdia

Mankidi and Mankirdias are actually the Birhors of Orissa. They are known differently in different areas. As per 1991 census, the population of Mankidi tribe is 1150 and that of Mankirdias 1491. Their lifestyle, culture, nomadic habit, traditional occupation, dependence on Siali fibre are similar to those of the Birhors. There are socio-cultural interactions and kinship relations among Birhors, Mankidi and Mankirdias.

47. Matya

Matyas are mostly found in Malkangiri and Dhenkanal districts. Very few of them are seen in Balasore, Ganjam and Cuttack districts. Their population as per 1991 census is 13226. Matyas live in adjacent areas inhabited by Bhumias and other communities. They are considered as younger brothers of Bhumias. Their life style, culture and socio-economic practices are similar to those of Bhumias. Matyas of Dhenkanal seem to be different from those of Malkangiri district in terms of their dialects, culture and lifestyle.

48. Mirdha

Mirdhas are known to be a tribe of Dravidian origin. They are found mainly in Bolangir and Sambalpur districts. Their traditional occupation is digging and carrying of earth. The word Mirdha means coolie. Mirdhas have become an agriculturist community with the passage of time. The community is divided into two sub-groups called Bada Kunhar and Sana Kunhar. The first group follows the customs of Kisan tribe whereas the second is more Hinduised. By and large, Mirdhas profess Hinduism and worship Gods and Goddess like Shiva, Vishnu, Durga, Mangla, Thakurani, etc. The total population of Mirdha tribe according to 1991 census is 30,982.

49. Mohali

Majority of Mohalis live in Sambalpur, Sundergarh and Mayurbhanj districts. According to 1991 census, their population is 13,585 with the females outnumbering the males. There are many similarities among Mohali, Santhal and Munda tribes because of their long association with each other. The economy of Mohalis is based on handicrafts and weaving. They usually sell their products in the local markets. Collection of minor forest produce, hunting and fishing are the means of their sustenance. Mohalis are considered to be migrants.

50. Munda

Mundas are a large tribe of Dravidian origin. Munda is a common term used by the Kols as the headman of village. It is a titular or functional designation used by the members of the tribe, as well as by outsiders. Traditionally, Mundas happened to be a wandering community. With the passage of time, they have become settled agriculturists. They are found more or less in all the districts of Orissa. They live along with other Kolarian tribes like Santhals, Kolhas, Hos, etc. Their total population according to 1991 census is 3.97 lakhs. The proportion of Munda population is the highest in Sundargarh. They live mainly in the northern and north-eastern part of the district.

51. Mundari

Mundaris are distributed in districts of Sundargarh, Mayurbhanj, Keonjhar, Balasore and adjoining areas. According to 1991 census, their total population is 3114 with the sex ratio favouring the females. The life-style and culture of Mundaris are almost similar to that of the Ho community. Indeed, they are considered to be a major section of the Ho tribe.

52. Omanatya

Omanatyas are agriculturists by occupation. They do not have a separate language or dialect. The term 'Omanatya' seems to be a distorted form of 'Amatya'. As the European officials could not pronounce indigenous terms correctly, they recorded names as per their comprehension and convenience. According to a popular legend, ancestors of this tribe were Ministers of Shri Rama at Ayodhya. After departure of Rama, they took to agriculture. The tribe is found mainly around Jaypore and Nawarangpur. According to 1991 census, Omanatya has a population of 25,915.

53. Oraon

This is a major tribe in the State with a population of 2.58 lakhs (1991 census). The female population (1.30 lakhs) is marginally higher than the male population (1.28 lákhs). Oraons principally inhabit Sundergarh and adjoining areas of Sambhalpur districts. According to a popular folk-tale, the first ancestor of the community arrived from the blood of the chest (Uras in Sanskrit) of a holy ascetic. To begin with, the community came to be known as Urager. Another folktale connects them with one of the ancient clans called Karakh. Their original mother tongue is still known as Kurukha, which is classified as a Dravidian language. Nowadays, they speak Sadri, which is a mixture of Hindi and various other dialects of Chota Nagpur plateau. Oraons are known as an agricultural community. A large section of their population is engaged in mining, processing servicing and industrial activities. They are also famous for their expertise in rural crafts and carpentry.

54. Parenga

Parengas are a colourful tribe of Koraput district. Despite their social traits and characteristics being similar to those of Gadabas, they are different. Parengas have their own language called Munda, which is comparable with the language spoken by Savaras of Parlakheanundi (Gajapati district). They mostly speak Telugu. Agriculture is their main occupation with shifting cultivation still in practice. The family income is supplemented by minor forest produce and raising vegetables. The total population of Parengas according to 1991 census is 5,843.

55. Paroja

This is one of the major well-known tribes of Orissa mostly found in Koraput and Kalahandi districts. It is seen sporadically in parts of Sundargrh, Keonjhar, Puri and Cuttack districts. The population of Paroja tribe as per 1991 census is 3.53 lakhs with the sex ratio in favour of the females. Parojas are divided into four main sections, namely, Bada Paroja or Sodia Paroja, Bad Jodia Paroja or Penga Paroja, Bareng Jodia Paroja and Konda Paroja or Selia Paroja. The Bada Paroja follow Hindu traditions and do not eat beef or buffalo meat. The community is more advanced economically. It claims higher position in the social hierarchy. Cross-cousin marriages are preferred and rules of the clan and village exogamy are rigidly followed. Agriculture is the mainstay and maize, millets, nizer, Ragi and paddy are the major crops grown by the community. Parojas also practise shifting cultivation.

56. Pentia·

Numerically, it is a small tribe mainly found in Koraput, Myurbhanj and Keonjhar districts. The total population of Pentias is 11,399 (1991 census). They live in villages located in plains in separate Hamlets. They are mainly settled agriculturists. Their position in the tribal society is quite high due to the process of Sanskritization. They follow the socio-cultural practices of caste Hindus and invite Brahmins priests for performing important rituals. Koya, paroja, Gadba, Bondo, Konds etc. are treated by them as inferior.

57. Rajuar

Rajuars are a small tribe, mostly found in Mayurbhanj district of Orissa. As per 1991 census their total population is 3146 with females accounting for more than 50 percent of the population.

58. Santal

Santals inhabit undulated and hilly regions of Mayurbhanj, Keonjhar and Balasore districts. Numerically, they are one of the largest tribes in the State with a population of 6.30 lakhs, according to 1991 census. Their language called Santhali belongs to Mundari group of Austric family. Traditionally, they used to wander from place to place for agricultural activities. They have now become permanent settlers in their existing habitations. Santals are divided into a number of clans namely Hansada, Murmu, Kisku, Hambrum, Marandi, Tudu, Soren, Baske, Basra, Pauria, Chane and Bedia. The last three clans are not found in Orissa. Agriculture is their mainstay and income dirived from it is supplemented by minor forest produce and wage earnings. Santals have undergone decades of socio-economic change and adjusted accordingly. The influence of Hinduism is evident in their socio-religious practices and caste system followed by them. They are highly assertive.

59. Saora

Saoras are known as one of the oldest tribes in Orissa spread over the southern districts of the State. Bulk of their population lives in Gajapati and Rayagada districts. Being one of the oldest tribes, references about Saoras are found in the Hindu mythology. The principal economic activity pursued by them is agriculture including shifting cultivation. The more advanced sections of the community have attained expertise in settled agriculture through terraced cultivation on the hill slopes. They draw water from the perennial and semi- perennial hill streams through indigenously constructed diversion weirs, check dams, etc., for irrigation purpose. The primitive sections of Saora tribe continue to subsist on shifting cultivation and minor forest produce. Two Micro Projects have been set up for their economic rehabilitation. The population of Saoras is 4.04 lakhs (1991 census) with the sex ratio favouring the females.

60. Shabar

Shabars are mainly distributed in coastal districts of the State. According to popular tales, a section of Saoras came to be known as Shabars after their migration to the coastal areas. They speak Oriya language and worship Hindu Gods and Goddesses which is a result of assimilation and upward mobility. Shabars are divided into two main sections called Jara Shabars and Vasu Shabars. The former claim to be descendant of king Jara, who was killed by Lord Krishna and the latter are said to be devotees of Lord Jagannath. They believe in life after death. The population of Shabars according to 1991 census is 3.74 lakhs with sex ratio in favour of the females.

61. Sounti

Sountis are found all over the State except in a couple of districts. However, their concentration is in the two districts, namely, Mayurbhanj and Keonjhar. Their population according to 1991 census is 96,251 with the females (49.791) outnumbering the males (46,460). Agriculture is the main occupation of Sountis. Those who do not possess land, work as farm labour and wage earners. Social festivals are observed by them as per the Hindu calendar and in the same manner as by their Hindu neighbours.

62. Tharua

Tharuas are found in Dhenkanal, Balagir, Balasore and Mayurbhanj districts of the State. Their population according to 1991 census is 1595. Very little is known about their socio-economic life and culture.

Other Unspecified Tribes

There are many tribes in the State which have yet to be listed in the relevant Constitution Order to get the benefits of protective measures and other special provisions meant for the Scheduled Tribes. The total population of such unlisted tribes in the State is 31,214 according to 1991 census.

Distribution of Scheduled Tribes in Orissa in terms of Rural, Urban, Male and Female with the districtwise details at Annexure I to XIII is given in the following table.

TABLE 4.1

DISTRIBUTION OF SCHEDULED TRIBE POPULATION BY SEX*

State	*Total/ Rural/ Urban*	*POPULATION*		
		Total	*Males*	*Females*
1	*2*	*3*	*4*	*5*
All Scheduled Tribes				
	Total	70,32,214	35,12,891	35,19,323
	Rural	66,70,506	33,25,442	33,45,064
	Urban	3,61,708	1,87,449	1,74,259
1. Bagata				
	Total	4,806	2,490	2,316
	Rural	4,547	2,338	2,209
	Urban	259	152	107
2. Baiga				
	Total	1,556	722	834
	Rural	1,472	688	784
	Urban	84	34	50
3. Banjara, Banjari				
	Total	12,843	6,279	6,564
	Rural	12,643	6,180	6,463
	Urban	200	99	101
4. Bathudi				
	Total	1,71,074	85,552	85,522
	Rural	1,65,399	82,430	82,969
	Urban	5,675	3,122	2,553
5. Bhottada, Dhotada				
	Total	3,04,137	1,36,387	1,67,750
	Rural	2,98,938	1,33,475	1,65,463
	Urban	5,199	2,912	2,287

(Continued on next page)

* Census Report 1991, Registrar General of India, New Delhi.

(Table 4.1 Contd.)

6. Bhuiya, Bhuyan				
	Total	2,46,573	1,21,951	1,24,622
	Rural	2,32,540	1,14,525	1,18,015
	Urban	14,033	7,426	6,607
7. Bhumia				
	Total	1,09,538	56,657	52,881
	Rural	1,08,917	56,361	52,556
	Urban	621	296	325
8. Bhumij				
	Total	1,78,214	89,852	88,362
	Rural	1,67,279	84,032	83,247
	Urban	10,935	5,820	5,115
9. Bhunjia				
	Total	11,276	5,709	5,567
	Rural	10,904	5,520	5,384
	Urban	372	189	183
10. Binjhal				
	Total	1,19,929	60,979	58,950
	Rural	1,07,781	54,758	53,023
	Urban	12,148	6,221	5,927
11. Binjhia, Binjhoa				
	Total	8,128	4,042	4,086
	Rural	7,076	3,581	3,495
	Urban	1,052	461	591
12. Birhor				
	Total	825	430	395
	Rural	641	343	298
	Urban	184	87	97
13. Bondo Poraja				
	Total	7,315	3,475	3,840
	Rural	7,268	3,452	3,816
	Urban	47	23	24

(Continued on next page)

(Table 4.1 Contd.)

14. Chenchu				
	Total	275	172	103
	Rural	247	146	101
	Urban	28	26	2
15. Dal				
	Total	19,867	9,821	10,046
	Rural	19,682	9,731	9,951
	Urban	185	90	95
16. Desua Bhumij				
	Total	1,880	1,014	866
	Rural	1,691	926	765
	Urban	189	88	101
17. Dharua				
	Total	11,512	6,367	5,145
	Rural	11,442	6,314	5,128
	Urban	70	53	17
18. Didayi				
	Total	5,471	2,694	2,777
	Rural	5,447	2,681	2,766
	Urban	24	13	11
19. Gadaba				
	Total	67,138	34,039	33,099
	Rural	63,776	32,182	31,594
	Urban	3,362	1,857	1,505
20. Gandia				
	Total	3,588	1,790	1,798
	Rural	3,482	1,719	1,763
	Urban	106	71	35
21. Ghara				
	Total	1,553	664	889
	Rural	1,339	576	763
	Urban	214	88	126

(Continued on next page)

(Table 4.1 Contd.)

22. Gond, Gondo				
	Total	7,01,139	3,50,375	3,50,764
	Rural	6,80,133	3,39,683	3,40,450
	Urban	21,006	10,692	10,314
23. Ho				
	Total	50,892	24,370	26,522
	Rural	48,545	22,950	25,595
	Urban	2,347	1,420	927
24. Holva				
	Total	13,662	6,481	7,181
	Rural	11,991	6,393	5,598
	Urban	1,671	88	1,583
25. Jatapu				
	Total	9,139	4,657	4,482
	Rural	8,669	4,359	4,310
	Urban	470	298	172
26. Juang				
	Total	35,665	17,320	18,345
	Rural	34,938	16,886	18,052
	Urban	727	434	293
27. Kandha Gauda				
	Total	19,278	10,080	9,198
	Rural	18,025	9,423	8,602
	Urban	1,253	657	596
28. Kawar				
	Total	9,582	4,721	4,861
	Rural	9,346	4,602	4,744
	Urban	236	119	117
29. Kharia, Kharian				
	Total	1,68,407	82,302	86,105
	Rural	1,51,991	74,278	77,713
	Urban	16,416	8,024	8,392

(Continued on next page)

(Table 4.1 Contd.)

30. Kharwar				
	Total	3,280	1,536	1,744
	Rural	3,058	1,404	1,654
	Urban	222	132	90
31. Khond, Kond, Kandha, Nanguli Kandha, Sitha Kandha				
	Total	11,40,374	5,77,850	5,62,524
	Rural	11,07,831	5,58,629	5,49,202
	Urban	32,543	19,221	13,322
32. Kisan				
	Total	2,66,371	1,33,272	1,33,099
	Rural	2,46,772	1,22,986	1,23,786
	Urban	19,599	10,286	9,313
33. Kol				
	Total	5,777	2,887	2,890
	Rural	4,959	2,497	2,462
	Urban	818	390	428
34. Kolah Loharas, Kol Loharas				
	Total	12,321	5,994	6,327
	Rural	11,051	5,410	5,641
	Urban	1,270	584	686
35. Kolha				
	Total	4,04,864	2,01,941	2,02,923
	Rural	3,87,684	1,92,871	1,94,813
	Urban	17,180	9,070	8,110
36. Koli, Malhar				
	Total	5,093	2,392	2,701
	Rural	4,413	2,085	2,328
	Urban	680	307	373
37. Kondadora				
	Total	19,235	10,498	8,737
	Rural	18,176	9,809	8,367
	Urban	1,059	689	370

(Continued on next page)

(Table 4.1 Contd.)

38. Kora				
	Total	10,313	5,575	4,738
	Rural	9,926	5,380	4,546
	Urban	387	195	192
39. Korua				
	Total	1,989	962	1,027
	Rural	1,645	831	814
	Urban	344	131	213
40. Kotia				
	Total	28,607	14,529	14,078
	Rural	28,372	14,418	13,954
	Urban	235	111	124
41. Koya				
	Total	1,41,927	73,966	67,961
	Rural	1,41,408	73,774	67,634
	Urban	519	192	327
42. Kulis				
	Total	6,526	3,245	3,281
	Rural	5,800	2,911	2,889
	Urban	726	334	392
43. Lodha				
	Total	7,458	3,650	3,808
	Rural	7,149	3,506	3,643
	Urban	309	144	165
44. Madia				
	Total	1,439	653	786
	Rural	1,278	567	711
	Urban	161	86	75
45. Mahali				
	Total	13,585	6,742	6,843
	Rural	12,283	6,143	6,140
	Urban	1,302	599	703

(Continued on next page)

(Table 4.1 Contd.)

46. Mankidi				
	Total	1,150	564	586
	Rural	1,046	498	548
	Urban	104	66	38
47. Mankirdia				
	Total	1,491	745	746
	Rural	1,455	727	728
	Urban	36	18	18
48. Matya				
	Total	13,226	6,528	6,698
	Rural	12,588	6,223	6,365
	Urban	638	305	333
49. Mirdhas				
	Total	30,853	15,982	14,871
	Rural	29,519	15,221	14,298
	Urban	1,334	761	573
50. Munda, Munda Lohara, Munda Mahalis				
	Total	3,96,561	2,00,389	1,96,172
	Rural	3,48,163	1,75,117	1,73,046
	Urban	48,398	25,272	23,126
51. Mundari				
	Total	31,147	15,101	16,046
	Rural	25,807	12,273	13,534
	Urban	5,340	2,828	2,512
52. Omanatya				
	Total	25,915	13,415	12,500
	Rural	25,549	13,238	12,311
	Urban	366	177	189
53. Oraon				
	Total	2,57,829	1,27,820	1,30,009
	Rural	2,17,673	1,07,753	1,09,920
	Urban	40,156	20,067	20,089

(Continued on next page)

(Table 4.1 Contd.)

54. Parenga				
	Total	5,843	3,017	2,826
	Rural	5,744	2,974	2,770
	Urban	99	43	56
55. Paroja				
	Total	3,53,336	1,73,127	1,80,209
	Rural	3,34,461	1,65,876	1,68,585
	Urban	18,875	7,251	11,624
56. Pentia				
	Total	11,399	6,212	5,187
	Rural	11,090	6,078	5,012
	Urban	309	134	175
57. Rajuar				
	Total	3,146	1,543	1,603
	Rural	2,866	1,408	1,458
	Urban	280	135	145
58. Santal				
	Total	6,29,782	3,21,436	3,08,346
	Rural	5,97,593	3,03,965	2,93,628
	Urban	32,189	17,471	14,718
59. Saora, Savar, Saura, Sahara				
	Total	4,03,510	2,00,261	2,03,249
	Rural	3,89,413	1,92,842	1,96,571
	Urban	14,097	7,419	6,678
60. Shabar, Lodha				
	Total	3,73,545	1,85,482	1,88,063
	Rural	3,57,987	1,77,406	1,80,581
	Urban	15,558	8,076	7,482
61. Sounti				
	Total	96,251	46,460	49,791
	Rural	94,142	45,326	48,816
	Urban	2,109	1,134	975

(Continued on next page)

(Table 4.1 Contd.)

62. Tharua				
	Total	1,595	872	723
	Rural	1,429	760	669
	Urban	166	112	54
63. Unclassified				
	Total	31,214	16,853	14,361
	Rural	26,027	14,004	12,023
	Urban	5,187	2,849	2,338

Note: 1. All Scheduled Tribes includes figures for 'unclassified'.
2. Tribes having nil return are not shown.

Linguistically, tribes in Orissa are broadly classified in three categories, namely, i) Indo-Aryan speakers, (Dhelki-Oriya, Matia, Haleb, Jharia, Saunti, Laria, and Oriya), 2) Dravidian (Pengo, Gondi, Kisan, Konda, Koya, Parji, Kui, Kuvi, and Kurukh or Oraon) and 3) Austric speakers (Birija, Perenga, Kisan, Bhumij, Koda, Mahili, Bhimiji, Mirdha-Kharia, Ollar Gadaba, Juang, Bondo, Didayee, Karmali, Kharia, Munda, Ho, Mundari and Savara).

The impact of modernization is not uniform among all the tribal communities. By and large, their economy is subsistence oriented being based on shifting cultivation, primitive agricultural practices, collection of minor forest produces, simple arts and crafts, cattle herding, etc. The social practices include community control over the common property resource, supernatural beliefs and practices. Migration of tribal population towards urban are industrialized regions is increasing progressively.

Scheduled Areas and Tribal Sub-Plan Areas in Orissa

The Scheduled Areas (States of Bihar, Gujarat, Madhya Pradesh and Orissa) Order, 1977, made in exercise of the powers conferred under sub paragraph (2) of paragraph 6 of the Fifth Schedule of the Constitution, specifies the following Scheduled Areas in the State of Orissa:

1. Mayurbhanj district.
2. Sundargarh district.
3. Koraput district (now divided into four districts).
4. Kuchinda tahsil in Sambalpur district.
5. Keonjhar and Telkoi tahsil of Keionjhar sub division, and Champua and Barbil tahsils of Champua sub division in Keonjhar district.
6. Khondmal tahsil of Khandmal sub division, and Balliguda and G. Udayagiri tahsils of Balliguda sub division in Boudh-Khondmal district (now the whole of Phulbani/Khondmal district).
7. R. Udayagiri tahsil, and Guma and Rayagada Blocks of Parlakhemundi tahsil of Parlakhemundi sub division (now the Gajapati district except Kashipur and Gosani Blocks) and Suruda tahsil excluding Gazalbadi and Gocha Gram Panchayats in Ghumsur sub division of Ganjam district.
8. Thuamul Rampur Block of Kalahandi tahsil and Langigarh Blocks falling in Lanjigarh and Kalahandi tahsils in Bhawanipatna sub division of Kalahandi district.
9. Nilgiri Block of Nilgiri tahsil in sub division, Balasore district.

About 45 per cent of the State's geographical area has been specified as Scheduled Areas. The Tribal Sub Plan Blocks identified for the socio-economic uplift of the tribal communities under the TSP Approach are coterminus with the Scheduled Areas except Suruda tahsil of Ganjam district. Considering the areas covered under ITDPs, Micro Projects, MADA Pockets and Clusters taken together, tribal population accounts for majority in about 50 per cent of the State's geographical area.

4.3. Initiatives for Tribal Development in Orissa

Among the major States under the Union of India, Orissa has the highest percentage of the Scheduled Caste and Scheduled Tribe population taken together. It is a well known fact that the communities notified as Scheduled Castes under the Constitution despite remaining part of the traditional social structure, had been victims of socio-economic discrimination for ages. Those designated as the Scheduled Tribes had not been integrated fully with the main-stream of the society. The development interventions initiated after independence have not been inadequate to place these communities on a par with their non-tribal counterparts. Indeed, this explains the economic backwardness of Orissa, as a whole. The strategy adopted for the development of tribals in the State has been the same as elsewhere in the Country. As explained earlier, the TSP approach conceived during the 5th Five-Year Plan was a well planned strategy to deal with the socio-economic backwardness of tribal people. This was supplemented by introducing 21 Integrated Tribal Development Project (ITDPs). The ITDPs, which took agency form subsequently, covered all the 118 tribal majority Blocks (out of 314 Blocks)' in the State. The details of ITDPs/ITDAs and TSP Blocks are shown in Tables 4.1 and 4.2.

TABLE 4.1
ITDPs/ITD in Orissa

Name of the District	*Name of the ITDP/ITDA*
1 Balasore	1 Nilgiri
2 Mayurbhanj	2 Baripada
	3 Rairangpur
	4 Karanjia
	5 Kaptipada
3 Sundargarh	6 Sundargarh
	7 Panposh
	8 Bonai
4 Sambhalpur	9 Kuchinda

5	Keonjhar	10	Keonjhar
		11	Champua
6	Gajapati	12	Parlakhemundi
7	Phulbani	13	Phulbani
		14	Balliguda
8	Kalahandi	15	Th. Rampur
9	Koraput	16	Koraput
		17	Jeypur
10	Malkangiri	18	Malkangiri
11	Nawarangpur	19	Nawarangpur
12	Rayagada	20	Rayagada
		21	Gunupur

TABLE 4.2
TSP Blocks in Orissa

Sl. No.	*District*	*I.T.D.P./ ITDA*	*Block undei*
1	*2*	*3*	*4.*
1.	Balasore	Nilgiri	Nilgiri
2.	Boudha Khondmals	Baliguda	Baliguda Nuagaon Kotagarh Daringbadi Tikabali G. Udayagiri Raikia Chakapada
3.	Phulbani		Phulbani Phiringia Khapuripada
4.	Ganjam	Paralakhemundi	R. Udayagiri Rayanguda Mohana Gumma Nuagada

(Continued on next page)

(Table 4.2 Contd.)

5.	Kalahandi	Th. Rampur	Th. Rampur
			Lanjigarh
6.	Keonjhar	Keonjhar	Patna
			Ghatagaon
			Keonjhar
			Saharpada
			Harichandanpur
			Telkoi
			Bansapal
		Champua	Champua
			Jhumpura
			Joda
7.	Koraput	Koraput	Koraput
			Laximipur
			Lamptapur
			Dasmanthpur
			Narayanpatna
			Bondhugaon
			Simliguda
			Pottangi
			Nandapur
		Rayagada	Rayagada
			Kalanara
			Kalyansinghpur
			Kanshipur
		Malkangiri	Malkangiri
			Balimela
			Govindapalli
			Kudumuliguma
			Mathili
			Kalimela-I
			KalimelaII
		Jeypore	Jeypore
			Boniguma
			Kotpad

(Continued on next page)

(Table 4.2 Contd.)

			Boipariguda
			Kundra
		Nowrangpur	Nowrangpur
			Tintalkhunti
			Papadahandi
			Kosagumuda
			Raighar
			Umerkota
			Chandahandi
			Jharigaon
			Dabugaon
			Nandahandi
		Gunupur	Gunupur
			Gudari
			Padmapur
			Ramanaguda
			Bissumcuttack
			Muniguda
			Chandrapur
8.	Mayurbhanj	Baripada	Baripada
			Badasahi
			Samakhunta
			Betanati
			Rasagovindapur
			Murda
			Bangiriposi-I
			Bangiriposi-II (Saraskama)
			Kuliana
			Sulipada
		Rairangpur	Bisoi-I
			Bijatola
			Kusumi
			Rairangpur
			Tiringi

(Continued on next page)

(Table 4.2 Contd.)

			Bahalda Jamada
		Karanjia	Karanjia Raruan Joshipur Thakumunda Sukuruli
		Kaptipada	Khunti-I Khunti-II Kaptipada Udala
9.	Sambalpur	Kuchinda	Kuchnda Govindapur Jamankira
9.	Sundergarh	Sundergarh	Sundergarh Subdega Balisankara Lefripada Baragach Tangarpali Hemagiri Kutna Rajgangpur
		Panposh	Kurrmunda Birra Nuagaon Bathiketa
		Bonai	Bonaigarh Lahunipada Gurunida Koira

Modified Area Development Approach (MADA)

Considering that a significant section of the tribal population remained in pockets outside the tribal sub-plan Blocks, a special programme was drawn to cover the contiguous villages having ten thousand population and above in the non-TSP Blocks with tribals accounting for 50 per cent or more. A programme known as the Modified Area Development Approach (MADA) was drawn for tribal families of such pockets. Accordingly, 46 MADA Pockets were been identified in the in the non-TSP Blocks of the State as shown in Table 4.3.

TABLE 4.3
Mada Pockets

Name of the district	Name of the MADA Pocket
1. Jaipur	1. Sukinda-I
	2. Sukinda-II
	3. Sukinda-III
	4. Danagadi
2. Khurda	5. Banapur Renapur
3. Nayagarh	6. Nuagaon
	7. Gania Daspalla
4. Baleswar	8. Jaleswar
5. Keonjhar	9. Anandapur-I
	10. Anandpur-II
	11. Hatadihi
	12. Ghasipura
6. Angul	13. Pallahara
7. Dhenkenal	14. Athamallick
8. Ganjam	15. Kankadahad
9. Gajapati	16. Turubudi
10. Boudh	17. Kashinagar
11. Bolangir	18. Boudh
	19. Khaprakhole
	20. Tureikela
	21. Tentulikhunti
	22. Deogaon Patnagarh
	23. Saintala Muribahal
12. Sambalpur	24. Dhanakauda
	25. Jujumura
13. Jharsuguda	26. Kolabira-Rengali
	27. Lakhanpur
	28. Jharsuguda Lakhanpur
	29. Laikera-Kirmira
14. Bargarh	30. Paikamal
	31. Paikamal-Jharbandh
15. Deogarh	32. Barkote
	33. Tileibani
16. Kalahandi	34. Bhawanipatna

	35. Kesinga
	36. Junagarh
	37. Madanpur-Rampur
	38. Jayapatna
	39. Narla
17. Nawapara	40. Komna
	41. Boden
	42. Nawapara-I
	43. Nawapara-II
	44. Khariar-I
	45. Khariar-II
	46. Sinapalli

Cultures

Further, smaller groups of villages in the non-TSP Blocks with a population of 5000 and above with the tribal population of 50 per cent or more have been identified as 'Clusters' and a programme similar to that of MADA was drawn focussing on the economic uplift of tribal families residing in those clusters. Fourteen such clusters as mentioned in Table 4.4 have been identified in the non-TSP Blocks.

TABLE 4.4
Cultures

Name of district	*Name of the Cluster*
1. Dhenkanal	1. Dhenkanal
2. Angul	2. Angul
3. Sambalpur	3. Naktideul
4. Bargarh	4. Padmapur
5. Bolangir	5. Belapada
6. Boudh	6. Kantamal
7. Ganjam	7. Suruda
	8. Sanakhemundi
8. Nuapada	9. Nuapada
9. Kalahandi	10. Koksara-I
	11. Koksara-II
	12. Jayapatna-II
10. Jajpur	13. Bhawanipatna
	14 . Barachana

Primitive Tribal Groups (PTG)

Another significant intervention towards the tribal development in the State was identification of the most Primitive Tribal Groups and special schemes for their socio-economic development keeping in view their specific needs. Thirteen Micro Projects as shown in Table 4.5 have accordingly been set up in the State as follows:

TABLE 4.5
Most Primitive Tribal Groups

Name of the district	*Name of the PTGs*
Sundergarh	1. Birhor
Malkangiri	2. Bonda Poraja
Malkangiri	3. Didayi
Malkangiri	4. Dongria Khond
Keonjhar	5. Juangs
Myurbhanj	6. Kharias
Phulbani, Kalahandi	7. Kutia Khond
Gajapate	8. Lanjia Souras
Myurbhanj	9. Lodhas
Myurbhanj	10. Mankidias
Anugool	11. Paudi Bhuyans
Gajapati	12. Soura
Nuapada	13. Chuktia Bhunjiya

The tribal families living in scattered villages and in urban areas not covered under the aforesaid programmes have been covered under the Dispersed Tribal Development Projects (DTDP).

It will be desirable to mention here that the programmes discussed above are over and above the normal plans and schemes wherein Scheduled Areas and Scheduled Tribes are expected to receive allocations for developmental programmes in proportion to the tribal population and considering the existing imbalance in tribal *vis-à-vis* non-tribal areas.

5

Critical Analysis of Tribal Development Administration

"Development" commonly refers to the overall improvement in the quality of life. Historically, most of the attempts for the promotion of development have been along the economic lines. The non-economic aspects of development received little attention of economists and social scientists until 1960s. In South (developing countries), it was sought to be brought by replicating the experience of North (developed countries), without taking into account, the social and regional factors. As a matter of fact, the United Nations declared the first "Development Decade" in early 1960s, aiming at a minimum annual economic growth of five and six percents for developed and developing countries, respectively.

The term "development" received a wider meaning in the terminology of the United Nations in 1970, when the ultimate purpose of development became equitable distribution of income and wealth by promoting social justice, along with the efficiency of production. The emphasis laid on the human element of development resulted in the conceptual emergence of "Social Development" with greater meaning and implication. Social Development till 1960s, was understood more in a social welfare and social service sense and was seen as the social dimension to more dominant economic basis of development. During the 1970s it referred to the process of planned institutional change to bring about a better correspondence between human needs on the one hand and social policies and programmes on the other (Jones, John F, p. 3, 1981).

Development Interventions

"Development Interventions" are considered to be the means of rapid social change to the benefit of rural populations, in a developing nation. Introduction of new ideas not only improves living standards through improved methods of production, but also facilitates transformation of the traditional society into a progressive one. The manifestation of development interventions in rural sector may be classified in the following forms:

1. Development of rural infrastructure, i.e., backward and forward linkages, followed by public and public utility services.
2. Development of natural resources like soil and water, etc., followed by implementation of beneficiary oriented income generating schemes.
3. Implementation of social welfare and social security schemes.
4. Human resource development.

The material benefits of the first three forms of development interventions are direct and tangible, whereas, the same cannot be held to be true in respect of human resources development. However, there is no dichotomy between the material and non-material factors and forms of development and both are complementary and contributory to the social development. In fact, the human resource development may be called to be a precondition for the development leading to the material benefits. Alternatively, material development, not being an end in itself, ultimately, leads to the non-material benefits, which can only be assessed in qualitative, subjective and spiritual terms.

Administration of schemes oriented towards material benefits is unlikely to be sustainable in the absence of certain critical non-material inputs among the intended beneficiaries. The goal of self-reliance and equality will remain distant, if the distribution of material benefits is attempted by way of development interventions, without cultivating non-material inputs. Moreover, the ultimate development of man, which is attainment of his creative potential, cannot be achieved by material benefits alone. The non-material benefits, attributable to the human resources development, play a vital part in the processes of social development.

Contribution of Education to Development

Education is fundamental to the social development. Illiteracy is invariably associated with deprivation and socio-economic under development. Realisation of this basic truth ultimately found expression in the resolution "Education for all" at the world conference on education held in March, 1990 at Jontien, Thailand. The vast literature of social science acknowledges education as the most important co-relate of development. Education enriches life and helps an individual to develop his personality. It is of special significance for rural masses, who are facing a new situation in the development process to adjust themselves to the changing conditions.

The role of education, as a direct investment, can be appreciated considering the spectacular recovery of war torn economy of Europe and Japan after the second world war. The fast reconstruction of the economy was based largely on the skill capital in these nations, which is indestructible over a short period. While a number of devices can be adopted for solving the problems of transition, sound foundation in a developing economy for sustained growth can be laid only through a system of universal education, upto a particular level. In the process of change, communication of ideas assumes a vital role. At the more local and practical level, education helps in breaking down the barriers on the way to change and assists the rural people to understand and adopt the new ideas, particularly, where these result in long term rather than immediate and more obvious benefits to the community (Batten, TR, p. 8,1959).

It has been confirmed through various studies that the children of illiterate parents, fall behind in scholastic achievement (Myrdal, G. 1970). One detrimental effect of an illiterate home begins in pre-school years, the formative stage of life, when attitudes are shaped and that would tend to persist. The educational programmes help to train the people to place responsibilities before rights. Education has also a determining influence on the rate at which economic progress is achieved and benefits which can be derived from it.

Economic development naturally makes growing demand on human resources and in a democratic set up it calls for values and attitudes in the building of which education plays a dominant part. Considering the contribution of education to the development and recognition of the right to learn, emphasis has to be made on its universal outreach, which co-relates to the development of the nation's economy. Thus, there is a nexus between universalisation of elementary education, continuing, non-formal and adult education.

A critical awareness through motivation, change of mentality and awareness contributes to the development of critical faculties in the rural oppressed people, leading them to the goal of liberation and social change (Freire, P. 1970). Increased attention is being drawn to the process of change in developing countries with greater emphasis on extension methods. Conscientisation as the potential of communication through written symbols and oral communication, may be understood in the same spirit through conscientised extension methodology. Extension education through different media, therefore, becomes an important element in the strategy of social development.

Social Development

Development without the motivation and full participation of the rural people has no foundation and no prospect of success, in the long run. The interrelation between participation and socio-economic development is always important. Participatory development, if fostered both in planning and implementation, would result in sustainability and empowerment, which are the key indicators of social development.

Social development in the form of empowerment, equitable distribution of income and wealth, is a far cry without creating a conducive atmosphere through awareness generation and skill development. Awareness, mobilisation and skill-training not only inculcate sense of protection and confidence in the rural women and other weaker sections, but also give them an opportunity to assert and play an important role in the socio-economic sphere. The awareness of gender equality, environmental degradation, health care, etc., is essential for the healthy growth of the society.

Social development without developing leadership qualities at the grass-root level results in distortions of various types. The consciousness gap between the rural masses and their leaders, who often do not belong to the area and rarely represent their will, goes against the interest of rural people. Development of leadership at the local level may eliminate the distortions of so-called popular representation.

Important of Material and Non-Material Benefits

Peace and coexistence; the supreme indicators and message of social development, cannot be felt without equality and respect for human rights. Mutual respect, tolerance and confidence lead the society to the perfection of development. Material development without respect for human rights, dignity and culture has the potential of leading the society to destruction, in addition to being incomplete and unsustainable. A society, irrespective of its material prosperity may disintegrate, as a result of unhealthy competition and suppression of human rights. Material benefits can satisfy the needs of the body, not the conscience.

Human resources development, mentioned above in different forms, has generally been regarded as a social service. It however, cannot be classified as a material factor and form of development. Neither, should it be bracketed with the public and public-utility services, though it does contribute to the material development. As already stated, the material and non-material dimensions of social development are closely inter-linked.

The non-material benefits can be said to be of greater importance as they are a pre-conditions of sustainable social development and to some extent, objectives too. However, they cannot be quantified. In fact, it would be futile to attempt to measure any country's social development, quantitatively and expect consensus about it as asserted by Mahboob-ul Haque: the world's richest may be considered to be its sickest and hence not developed at all.

Development Interventions : Isolationism Vs Assimilation

Historically, there appear to be two different schools of thought for the development of tribals: (a) Isolationism and (b) Assimilation through development interventions. The Colonial Administration and Anthropologists favoured the first, while the Administration during the post independence era tried to follow the latter.

Initially the Colonial administration tried to superimpose their conventional administrative system in the tribal areas. When they faced hostility from tribals, they started following a segregative and divisive policy in the name of non-intervention. This is evident from the fact that they did not object to the activities of Missionaries engaged in the spread of Christian propaganda despite publicly professing the policy of isolation (Ghurye, 1959:149-50).

The Anthropologists wanted "isolationism" to preserve the life style and culture of the tribals losing sight of the fact that the comparative isolation of tribals in the forests was nothing different from the early history of the entire human society. Elwin Verrier, an eminent anthropologist, had advanced an idea of a National Park for tribals(1939:515).

From the inception of planned development and introduction of the Community Development programmes, special multipurpose blocks were set up for the development of tribals. However, the policy on tribal development in the initial years remained excessively influenced by anthropologists, who had their own romantic views on the Tribal World of development. In 1959, a Committee was set up under the chairmanship of Elwin Verrier to study the progress of development in selected special multi-purpose blocks through out the country. The Committee submitted its report in March 1960 (Report of the Committee on Special Multipurpose Tribal Blocks), suggesting for a 'tribal touch' or 'tribal bias' in conceiving the policy and implementing the developmental programmes in tribal areas. The Committee, however, did not indicate in specific and descriptive terms as to what was meant by the "tribal touch"! It merely explained that "tribal touch" or "tribal bias" meant looking at things through tribal eyes and from the tribal point of view, recognise and respect their way of doing things (P.29, 1960). The report pleaded more for research and preservation of tribal art, tradition, culture, religions and traditional council, etc., instead of imposing development in it's various manifestations to be assessed in quantifiable physical and financial terms.

By and large, the tribal situation after independence, has been handled with a two pronged approach. The two dimensions of this approach as discussed in the previous chapter are: "protection" and "development". In the initial years of planned economy, tribal development remained part of the overall development strategy with limited additional outlay provided under backward classes sector. However, with the introduction of the TSP approach from the Fifth Five Year Plan onwards, the investment took a quantum jump as apparent Table 5.1 shows the percentage outlay for development in the various Five Year Plans.

TABLE 5.1
Plan Outlays of Tribal Development

Sl. No.	*Plan Period*	*Percentage of the total plan outlay*
1.	1st	1
2.	2nd	0.9
3.	3rd	0.6
4.	4th	0.5
5.	5th	3
6.	6th	5
7.	7th	9

(Figures are quoted from the WGRs for 7th and 8th plan: p. 2 & 15, respectively).

There is no doubt that considerable sums of money have been spent in the field of tribal welfare during the successive plan periods, though it is difficult to measure with accuracy, the success in the implementation of programmes formulated for the social and economic development of tribals. The disparity continues, if the progress is to be judged by what remains to be done to bring the tribals on a par with the rest of the population. The tribals have not been able to receive the desired benefits of development and protective legal provisions, largely due to their educational backwardness, lack of general awareness and suitable infrastructure. Besides, some inadequacies are manifest in the implementation of Protective Legislations, Developmental Programmes and Social Welfare schemes as the ensuing pages of the chapter will elaborate.

Protective Legislation and Tribals

Landholding Patterns

Most of the legislations are intended to ensure that tribal land does not pass on to the non-tribal through illegal and fraudulent transactions. None of the laws have recognised the customary rights and laws of tribal communities, which had a determining influence in the management of land in tribal areas from time immemorial. Traditionally, in most tribal areas, individual right of enjoyment of land and land based resources are embedded in communal systems of access to and management of resources. While in some of the tribal areas, feudal control was imposed on communal system, during the later part of the Colonial past, such attempts mostly remained on paper due to lack of administrative and productive infrastructure. In the post independence period, rather than correcting the distortions, they were accepted as crucial elements of the legal framework for implementation of policies and programmes in the tribal areas. Laws which existed on paper during the Colonial dispensation were recognised as such, over the laws on the ground, by which the people lived by and large, and still live their life.

It is not difficult to come across the dispossession of tribals that has taken place as a result of state policy regarding their customary rights. Only a fraction of the land, under possession of the tribals for generations has legally been recorded in their favour. They have been treated as encroachers in respect of land on which trees were planted by them and their forefathers. What makes the matter worse is the use of so-called scientific methods of land survey and concern for protection of environment as the justification of these anomalies.

Although the Revenue laws and regulations passed by various States, do provide for the prevention of illegal transfer of tribal land into the hands of non-tribals, the overall legal and administrative mechanism does not seem to be in favour of tribals. The declining size of tribal land holding in different States has already found place in various studies. The findings of the Agriculture Census 1985, in Orissa State, are revealing, as evident in the Table 5.2.

TABLE 5.2

Changing Land Holding Patterns of Tribals
(A case of Orissa)

Total cultivable land that belongs to Tribals, 1981-82	*Total cultivable land that belongs to Tribals, 1980-81*	*Average size of holding, 1980-81*	*Average size of holding, 1985-86*
1.58 million hectares	1.54 million hectares	1.7 hectares	1.6 hectares

(Agriculture Census Report, Orissa, 85-86:28-29).

The Village Forests in tribal areas despite being under communal control for generations, have been brought under the control of State. The Customary laws relating to communal control over the agricultural land and land under shifting cultivation has not been recognised in most of the States. The rules of Survey and Settlement in some States do not permit preparation of record of rights on the land above 10 degree slope, despite cultivation of such land by tribals for generations. The Survey and Settlement operation usually receives little priority in tribal areas. Ironically, whenever taken up, it means confiscation of tribal rights on the land above 10 degree slope. In the event of displacement on account of big irrigation projects, industrial and mining complexes, etc., tribal families in possession of land for generations do not receive fair amount of compensation and rehabilitation assistance simply because they do not possess official records of rights for no fault of their own.

There is hardly any participation of tribals in the management of forests. Although the National Forest Policy of 1988 provides for recording of all the forest land in possession of tribals prior to the enactment of the Forest Conservation Act 1980, the conditions laid therein for formalising the rights of tribal land holders are difficult to fulfil. No records in respect of the forest land under the possession of tribals can be prepared without arranging equal quantity of compensatory forests and approval of the Government of India. Moreover, the stipulation of up to 10 degree slope only is another barrier in some States. The officers of Forest Department show little concern for the cause of tribals, their primary responsibility being protection and enhancement of forest coverage. The tribals are in no position to create a situation to take the positive provisions of the protective laws to the logical end.

Although Government has been providing financial assistance to the weaker sections, for development of land, irrigation, etc., under various poverty alleviation schemes, the tribal cultivators are unable to take full advantage of such assistance, not being in a position to produce their rights and titles over the land to be developed. Implementation of Revenue laws and regulations, prohibiting alienation of tribal land, minimum wages provision and money lending, etc, is far from satisfactory.

Control on Moneylending Operations

The Working Group Report on the development of tribals during the 7th Five Year Plan quotes a benchmark survey report (p. 61) according to which, money lending as individual profession is still flourishing in tribal blocks of Maharashtra, Orissa and Rajasthan, notwithstanding substantial proliferation of the branches of Cooperatives and Commercial Banks. Another study by JHM Jones (1993, Ph. D. thesis) in a tribal village of Dungarpur district in Rajasthan reveals similar findings. The pernicious correlation between money lending and debt bondage is well known. Ironically, even the tribal members of the Cooperatives also tend to approach the illegal moneylenders for debt.

Developmental Programmes and Tribals

Development of Agriculture

Ninety eight percent of the tribals live in the rural areas and agriculture and allied activities constitute the mainstay for 93% of them (WGR, 1980-85: 69). By and large they live in the inhospitable terrains with depleted resources and sub marginal land. Very little of fertile valley and plain lands are in their possession. The chief crops grown by them on the sloppy and undulating land are millet, oil seeds and pulses. The level of irrigation is very low. Most of the precipitation wastes away in run-off because of poor quality of soil; lacking water conservation capacity. Shifting cultivation and dry upland farming are traditionally the most important sources of livelihood for some tribal communities even today, though overwhelming majority has taken to terraced and settled cultivation as the primary source of their livelihood.

The overall efforts for the development of agriculture in tribal areas have been based upon the patterns of more developed area without recognising the needs of the tribals, agro-climatic conditions, traditional agronomic practices and cultural constraints. Instead of subjecting new technology and agricultural practices of tribals to adaptive research and scrutiny with reference to acceptability and assimilation, the agricultural extension services of the Government seem to have tried to apply the ways and means adopted elsewhere, to the tribal areas also; almost ineffectively and half-heartedly. The contrast between the productivity level of 4 relatively developed non-tribal districts of Cuttack, Ganjam, Puri and Balasore and the four tribal districts ie. Koraput, Sundargarh and Keonjhar of Orissa (1980-81) can be seen in Table 5.3.

TABLE 5.3
Agricultural Productivity in Tribal and Non-Tribal Districts (A case of Orissa)

Sl.No.	*District*	*Gross value of output (Rs. In million)*	*Net area sown (000 hectares)*	*Gross value of output (per hectare)*
1.	Cuttack	3199	697	4590
2.	Ganjam	1993	500	3986
3.	Puri	1771	477	3713
4.	Balasore	1515	436	3475
5.	Sundargadh	652	274	2382
6.	Keojhar	644	286	2252
7.	Koraput	2082	863	2412

(Indicators of Economic Development IED), Orissa, 1992: 9).

It is further to be indicated that agricultural production in the first four predominantly non-tribal districts is affected adversely during the kharif season due to cyclone and flood. The last three predominantly tribal districts do not have comparable irrigation facility, still they are less prone to the natural calamities despite precipitation being quite high for agricultural operation. The productivity as mentioned above is very much less than that of non-tribal districts.

Although tribal areas are highly suitable for crops like maize, minor millet, pulses and agro-forestry schemes, negligible efforts have been made for greater intensity of such crops. The Training and Visit (T&V) system is yet to benefit the tribal farmers in the same way as others. The research and development work in the field of agriculture brought Green Revolution and self-sufficiency in respect of food grains production, but made little impact on the rain-fed land cultivated by less advanced tribal farmers. No attention worth mentioning was paid to develop and popularise the high yielding varieties of the traditional tribal crops.

Most of the efforts towards development of marketing infrastructure including the minimum support price for agricultural produces have remained directed at the non-tribal farmers of fertile areas. The tribal farmers have little options but to sell their produce at low prices due to lack of storage facilities. The use of fertilizers and chemical is minimum in the tribal areas even under irrigated conditions due to non-availability on account of poor transport and communication system and lack of access to the institutional credit. Lack of servicing centres in the tribal areas act as a disincentive to tribal farmers to take to improved agricultural implements.

The tribal areas offer a variety of agro-climatic zones where different types of fruits, vegetables, flower-species and medicinal plants, etc., can grow. Already wild fruit trees like jack-fruits, *aonla, ber, mahua, kendu, mayo, guava, banana, jamun,* citrus fruits, etc., are available in plenty. These could be converted into good commercial crops through improved techniques of horticulture and marketing support.

Soil Conservation

Soil conservation measures have not received attention in the tribal areas to the desired extent. Land management improvements have a direct and immediate bearing on productivity in addition to their long term significance in establishing the natural resource base. Despite existence of large number of perennial and semi-perennial streams and watersheds in the tribal areas, systematic attempts are yet to be made to utilize them. Land development including bench terracing is essential for settled cultivation and enhancing the moisture retention capability of land. Measures like gully control, vetiver bonding, diversion channels, sisal plantation and treatment of watersheds with the involvement of tribal farmers have to be popularised for suitable agricultural development in tribal areas.

Irrigation Programme

Despite considerable potential, the irrigation programme has not picked up in tribal areas. Due to hilly and undulating nature of land, tribal regions are suitable for minor irrigation projects, whereas major and medium irrigation projects normally get priority in the plan programmes. The major irrigation projects generally submerge tribal areas while they benefit the developed areas. Although some provisions have been made to settle the displaced families in the command area of the proposed irrigation projects, but due to lack of on-farm development and primitive methods of subsistence-agriculture followed by tribals, they hardly get any advantage of the rehabilitation package offered to them. Irrigated agriculture being capital intensive, tribal farmers are unable to take up cultivation of high yielding varieties due to lack of resources. Irrigated agriculture, backed by input and technical support is however, attracting the tribal communities towards settled cultivation, rapidly.

The land under irrigation in tribal areas is extremely low, despite some conscious efforts after the introduction of TSP approach. A comparison between the TSP and non-TSP districts of Orissa (1980-81) may be relevant to know the existing level of disparity in the field of irrigation development. The first four districts in Table 5.4 are non-TSP districts. Most of the irrigated land even in the TSP districts of Sundargarh, Keonjhar, and Koraput is owned by the non-tribals. The situation is identical in the other TSP States.

TABLE 5.4
DevelopEment of Irrigation in Tribal Districts (A case of Orissa)

Sl. No.	*Districts*	*Net Irrigated Area (000 hectares)*	*Net Area Sown (000 hectares)*	*Percentage of net area irrigated to net area sown*
1.	Cuttack	231	697	33.13
2.	Ganjam	247	500	49.4
3.	Puri	202	477	42.36
4.	Balasore	86	436	19.72
5.	Koraput	33	863	3.82
6.	Sundargarh	20	274	7.30
7.	Keonjhar	24	286	8.39

(IED, Orissa, 1992: 8).

Control Over Financial Exploitation

The TSP approach was conceived to achieve the twin objectives of socio-economic development of tribals and termination of exploitation. As exploits by moneylenders leading to chronic debt and bondage of tribals could not be eliminated only by passing laws and regulations without being backed by strong and sustained measures, credit and marketing had to be given high priority, both as protective as well as developmental measures.

More than 2500 Large Sized Multi-Purpose Cooperative Societies (LAMPS) had been set up in tribal areas (WGR, 1985-90: 110) to perform the three-fold functions of (a) purchase of surplus farm and forest produce; (b) sale of consumer necessities and farm inputs; and (c) provision of consumption and production credits . In addition to Cooperatives, Commercial Banks including Regional Rural Banks also started opening their branches in the tribal areas to extend credit under various Government sponsored priority sector schemes at a differential rate of interest.

The introduction of the formal finance however, did not deliver results to the desired extent. The mismanagement of Cooperatives which were superimposed by Government uniformly, without studying the ground realities, became obvious after erosion of their initial capital base. The bureaucratic functioning of Commercial and Rural Banks gave little relief to the poor tribals except under the poverty alleviation schemes; as if under compulsion. A Committee set up by the Reserve Bank of India (1981) to review institutional credit for agriculture and rural development analyzed the performance of Cooperatives in the tribal areas in the following words:

> "The LAMPS organised in tribal areas numbering 1824 have not been able to make satisfactory progress for reasons such as lack of aggressive investment lending, non-availability of trained and experienced personnel for manning executive positions, frequent increase in royalties payable on forest produce, unhealthy competition from the private traders, absence of effective marketing organisation and marketing intelligence, lack of infrastructural arrangements for storage and transportation and inadequacy of agency, commission paid to the societies for distribution activities" (WGR, 1985-90: 111).

Negative Side of Industrial Development

Large number of industrial and mining complexes have been set up in the mineral and raw-material rich tribal belts in the recent decades. The impact of industrial development on the tribals has been negative to a great extent, is evident from the observation made by the Working Group during the 6th Five Year Plan as follows :

> "A hoary agro-forest traditional culture has been confronted with a modern, sophisticated industrial culture. The abrupt juxtaposition has produced deleterious results for tribals. There has been large scale alienation of tribal land for the public and private sector industrial and mining complexes, township development etc. Having lost the basic resource, the tribals have not been able to secure sources of livelihood. The first generation has found it nearly impossible to imbibe the skills and culture of the industrial age. The shock impulses generated on account of the imposition of the modern industry have been beyond the absorption capacity of the tribal communities. In fact for the first generation, it has been an unmitigated disaster, in as much as it has meant nearly whole sale destitution. The question whether industrialisation planned for the placid tribal should not contend with the human sacrifice involved, acquires significance" (WGR: 92).

Infrastructure Development in TSP Areas

It is a hard fact that tribal areas are deficient in the field of infrastructure development compared to non-tribal areas. Villages in the TSP areas are widely dispersed and lack in all weather road communication system. This is one of the reasons for the socio-economic isolation of tribals. The Scheduled Areas and Scheduled Tribes Commission in their report observed that "development of communication will provide greater opportunity for the tribal to develop his national consciousness. He is essentially a rural entity. On no account, should he be drawn away from his native soil to hold out a morbid picture of uprooted humanity. Development programmes aimed at his all round progress including communication should therefore start with the village as the centre" (WGR, 1985-90: 158).

The geographical conditions of the TSP areas demand construction of large number of bridges and roads to make the communication all weather. Considering the fact that road communication provides access to educational facilities beyond the primary level, enables inward movement of essential commodities, generates wage employment and increases direct contact with Government and marketing agencies, it is imperative to develop suitable road communication system in the tribal areas. Unfortunately, the development of infrastructure did not receive adequate attention of the policy makers in the initial years of the planned intervention. The reliance on the anthropologist sponsored views of tribal development was responsible for the limited initiative, to a great extent. The situation improved to some extent, after introduction of the TSP concept.

Quantification of Funds for Tribal Development

The TSP approach stipulates for quantification of funds; not below the percentage of tribal population from the State Plan. The Union Ministries are required to make budget provisions for the development of tribals under a separate head as per guidelines. While most State Governments followed the stipulations of the TSP approach in principle, the Central Ministries never acted upon them. The plan provisions made by State Governments also remained notional, by and large. Moreover, earmarking of funds as per percentage of tribal population, was not enough to develop the essential infrastructure in the tribal areas, which had been ignored in the past. The quantification of funds under infrastructure sector should have been done considering the existing disparities between TSP and non TSP regions and total geographical area identified as the Sub Plan.

A careful study of the investment made under infrastructure sector would show that the major portion of the plan outlay earmarked under TSP head has been spent either for industrial and mining complexes or for road communication network around the mineral rich areas, which in fact, has resulted in the displacement of tribals. This is clear from the fact that the two Sub Plan districts of Orissa, i.e. Sundergarh and Koraput (having more than 55% tribal population each), occupy the last two places in the agricultural productivity, whereas the same two districts rank 1st and 4th in terms of industrial development (IED,1986: 8-12). Table 5.5 shows the coverage of surfaced road per thousand Sq. kms. in the TSP and non-TSP districts of Orissa State(1980-81). The better position of Sundergarh district is obviously due to the existence of a Steel Plant and large number of ancillaries developed around it. The districts holding 11th, 12th and 13th ranks, in addition to Sundargarh are TSP districts.

TABLE 5.5

Development of Road Communication (A case of Orissa)

Sl.No.	*Districts*	*Length of Road in kms.*	*Total area (sq. kms.)*	*Surface Road per 1000 sq. kms.*	*Rank*
1.	Balasore	735	6.39	115	5
2.	Cuttack	1511	11.21	155	2
3.	Ganjam	1978	12.53	154	1
4.	Puri	1252	10.16	123	5
5.	Dhenkanal	1156	10.83	107	7
6.	Bolangir	863	8.90	97	10
7.	Keonjhar	914	8.24	111	6
8.	Sundargarh	1252	9.67	130	4
9.	Phulbani	912	11.07	82	11
10.	Mayurbhanj	1059	10.41	102	8
11.	Sambalpur	1720	17.57	98	9
12.	Kalahandi	725	11.84	61	12
13.	Koraput	1441	27.02	53	13
	State	15520	155.84	100	

(IED, Orissa, 1992: 18).

Development of infrastructure determines the effectiveness of public and public utility services. It also influences the administration of social services and social welfare schemes. Although, the national norms have been relaxed for opening of schools, health centres and retail outlets in tribal areas, the reality in practice does not conform to the objectives due to lack of supporting infrastructure. The net result is bound to be far from satisfactory. It is unfair to allow the tribals to remain isolated and discriminated in the name of preserving their culture and protecting them from exploitation, which the development of road communication is suspected to entail. Instead of raising the question of demand and supply while talking of development needs in tribal areas, positive attempts have to be made to create demands by raising awareness and building requisite infrastructure. The implementation of protective legislation without creating a conducive atmosphere and required infrastructure is likely to remain a distant and far cry.

Large number of tribal habitations have remained without safe drinking water, school buildings, health centres and extension services, etc., due to lack of accessibility. They have remained untouched by Government agencies and Non Government Organisations alike. Rail and tele-communication systems, which are considered essential linkages for development, are yet to benefit the tribals like other segments of the society. Prescribing a different paradigm of development for tribals which has not been replicated anywhere else, amounts to open discrimination against the already isolated and marginalised communities.

Social Welfare Schemes and Tribals

Health and Nutrition

One of the major problems of the tribal communities is lack of adequate nutrition. There had been a time when the tribal areas had plenty of vegetables, fruits and animal resources. The tribal communities were earning enough to meet their needs through communal farming and shifting cultivation as the "land-man ratio" was not unfavourable in their areas. As a result of population growth, industrialisation and encroachment by outsiders, not only the traditional resource base of tribals has depleted, but they have also been exposed to the diseases unknown to them. Besides, they have been losing hold over indigenous medicines and techniques of preventive as well as curative treatments.

No systematic study has been conducted to understand the dimensions of health hazards faced by tribals despite accepting the prevalence of diseases such as malaria, leprosy, goitre, tuberculosis, anaemia, etc., in the tribal areas. Neither any initiative has been taken to know the medicinal herbs and plants traditionally used by tribals. In so far as coverage by health institutions in tribal areas is concerned, national norms have been relaxed for establishment of Primary Health Centres (PHC) and Sub Centres during the Seventh Plan (1985-90). A PHC can be established in tribal areas to cover a population of 20,000 as against 30,000 in the non-tribal areas. Similarly, a Sub Centre can be set up for a population of 3,000 in the tribal areas as against 5,000 in other areas. According to the figures available (WGR, 1990-95), the average population coverage by PHCs and Sub Centres in the tribal *vis-a-vis* non tribal areas during 1988-89 is as shown in Table 5.6.

TABLE 5.6

Primary Health Centres (PHCs) and Sub Centres in the TSP and TSP Area

Sl. No	*Name of the Area*	*Population Coverage, per PHC*	*Population Coverage per Sub Centre*
1.	TSP Area	37,000	5300
2.	Non TSP Area	53,000	6500

Although this average favours the tribal areas, but it ignores the facts of low population density, long distances, and difficult terrains in TSP areas due to which large number of health institutions remain inadequately staffed. The poor coverage of services is one of the factors influencing the Infant Mortality Rates (IMRs) in tribal areas. The figures of IMR available in respect of some of the TSP States (1979) are as shown in Table 5.7. (WGR, 1990-95):

TABLE 5.7

Infant Mortality Rate (IMR)

Sl. No.	*States*	*Rural IMR*	*Tribal IMR*
1.	Andhra Pradesh	120	144
2.	Gujarat	127	145
3.	Karnataka	81	82
4.	Maharashtra	84	98

Most of the TSP districts have been covered under the Universal Immunisation Programme(UIP) and Integrated Child Development Services (ICDS) in recent years, which has improved the health, referral services and nutrition level of tribal children and pregnant and nursing mothers; despite some operational problems in the implementation.

Provision of Education

Education is fundamental to the socio-economic development of any community as illiteracy is invariably associated with deprivation and socio-economic underdevelopment. The vast literature of social science acknowledges education as the most important correlate of development.

For the tribal communities, who at a very critical stage of their history are facing a new situation to adjust themselves to the change, education is of special significance.

Due to lack of access to education in the past, tribals are in a position of handicap in dealing with the present day administrative system. Economic development makes a growing demand on human resources and in a democratic set up, it calls for values and attitudes, in the building of which education plays a dominant part. The concept of rural social development through methods like conscientization, critical awareness, participation, group approach, etc., is unlikely to sustain without a minimum level of education. Tribal communities can not meet the challenges on terms of some degree of equality without being equipped with the modern formal education.

Theoretically, Governmental efforts in the field of tribal education have been towards removal of disparity between tribals and non-tribals. In practice however, educational development has been given a low priority. Table 5.8 gives, a comparison of progress in literacy percentage during the last five decades–1931 to 1981 (WGR, 1985-90: 145).

TABLE 5.8

Growth in Tribal and Non-tribal literacy

Sl. No.	*Census Year*	*Total Literacy*	*Tribal Literacy %*
1.	1931 Census	7.5%	0.75%
2.	1961 Do.	28.29%	8.54
3.	1971 Do.	34.5%	11.29%
4.	1981 Do.	36.20%	16.35%

The rates of drop-outs and forced-outs is very high among the school going children of tribal communities as the siblings start helping their parents for subsistence from the formative stage itself. Besides, there is no conducive atmosphere at home. The other problems in the promotion of education in tribal areas are: sparseness of population, small size of habitation and difficulties of communication. Although some residential schools, known as "Ashram Schools" have been established in the tribal areas, in addition to providing stipends to the tribal day scholars, the available educational infrastructure in tribal areas is grossly inadequate to meet the requirement of elementary education.

With the exception of four North Eastern tribal majority states of Nagaland, Meghalaya, Arunachal Pradesh and Mizoram, tribals in the rest of the country rank at the bottom in respect of educational development. While the National Policy on education envisages access to Lower Primary School (LPS) within a walking distance of one km., and Upper Primary School (UPS) within three kms., the objective has remained a far cry in the educationally backward tribal areas. A comparative study of three most advanced districts with the minimum tribal population *vis-a-vis* three most backward districts with predominantly tribal population would show the deficiency of educational infrastructure along with the correlate of education with development, in the State of Orissa as follows. The first three districts have tribal population of about 3 per cent each:

TABLE 5.9

Educational Infrastructure and Illiteracy and Poverty (A case of Orissa)

Sl. No.	*Districts*	*Literacy %(1981)*	*ST Population %*	*Average area (sq. km.) under each Lower primary school*	*Average area (sq. km.) under each Upper primary school*	*Average area (sq. km.) under each High school*	*Population % below the poverty line approx. figures of 1990*
1.	Cuttack	45.43	3.31	1.80	5.20	9.10	30
2.	Puri	45.40	3.45	3.00	9.10	15.10	30
3.	Balasore	42.00	6.84	2.20	4.8	8.90	30
4.	Koraput	16.13	55.22	5.20	46.10	101.90	70
5.	Kalahandi	19.42	31.21	4.90	32.00	48.20	70
6.	M. Bhanj	25.71	57.70	3.70	14.10	27.20	70

(The figures mentioned above have been quoted from the Census report 1981, and information furnished by the Department of Education and Panchayat Raj basing upon which a report on Tribal Education has been prepared).

The problem of infrastructural weakness in respect of the educational administration in the tribal regions has been admitted by the State Education Department of Orissa in the discussion paper prepared for the UNDP sponsored workshop to consider the project "Universal Outreach of Literacy by 2000 AD", as follows:-

"Important problems of education in tribal districts are non-availability of minimum facilities for primary and upper primary education. Till date (April 1992), children in the age group of 6-11 years belonging to more than 7,000 habitations out of 24,185 of the project area (which consists of four tribal districts), are deprived of primary schooling facilities within one km.distance and near about 50 per cent of habitations of the total project area have no upper primary schooling facilities within 3 kms distance. More than 2,700 primary institutions are building-less. There are 3,500 institutions which are single roomed schools out of which 2,700 are single teacher schools. Lack of access and non-availability of minimum teaching learning facilities, lead to non-enrolment and large number of forced-outs and drop-outs among the children in the age group of 6-11 and 11-14" (p. 18-19).

Added to this is the problem of modern education, alien to the tribal communities, which is being imparted in the language unknown to them. The situation is similar in other States with the exception of the north eastern tribal majority States. The literacy growth among tribals continues to be lower due to lack of infrastructure in the tribal areas is evident from the fact the 1991 census report:

TABLE 5.10

Comparative Literacy in Orissa according to 1991 census

Sl. No.	*District*	*Leteracy per cent*	*ST popu-lation %*	*Overall Literacy per cent*		*ST Literacy per cent*	
				Male	*Female*	*Male*	*Female*
1.	Cuttack	63.28	3.30	75.74	50.38	29.02	6.89
2.	Balasore	58.78	7.06	72.55	44.57	29.14	7.14
3.	Puri	63.82	3.52	76.82	49.94	45.06	13.83
4.	M. Bhanj	37.88	58.37	51.84	23.68	37.74	10.50
5.	Sundargarh	52.97	52.35	65.41	39.60	50.13	24.52
6.	Sambalpur	49.38	27.81	64.64	33.55	47.24	16.09
7.	Bolangir	39.74	18.79	57.26	21.88	41.49	9.03
8.	Keonjhar	44.73	45.07	58.00	30.00	38.01	11.74
9.	Dhenkanal	53.22	12.31	68.23	37.34	37.41	10.17
10.	Ganjam	44.26	9.52	60.77	28.09	27.64	6.82
11.	Kalahandi	30.05	31.36	45.54	14.56	32.00	5.38
12.	Koraput	22.66	54.87	32.15	13.09	15.68	2.39
13.	Phulbani	38.64	37.86	56.92	20.26	44.54	11.26
	Total	49.09	22.31	63.09	34.68	34.44	10.21

The educational backwardness among the tribals is the result of non-availability of suitable infrastructure and conducive atmosphere at home, the two key components of modern formal education. The immediate need is therefore for the opening of a large number of residential schools in the remote tribal areas. A study on Tribal Education in Orissa, reveals that the rates of drop-outs in the residential schools controlled by the Tribal Welfare Department in Orissa is up to 10 per cent against upto 90 per cent in the non-residential schools controlled by the State Education Department. A survey of successful tribal students in the matric examination shows that the rate of success has been much higher in the residential schools under reference, compared to the general schools. Table 5.11 substantiates the survey results.

TABLE 5.11
Performance of Tribal Students Reading in the Residential Schools (A case of Orissa)

Sl. No.	*Year*	*Total % of Successful students from all Schools T W Department*	*Percentage of Tribal Students from the Residential Schools of TW Department*
1.	1991	42.91	65.62
2.	1992	43.41	66.23
3.	1993	49.65	61.42

(The figures are based on the information received from the Board of Secondary Education, Orissa).

Another defect in the field of educational administration is the multiplicity of Governmental organisations running educational institutions in tribal areas. Although the limited number of Ashram Schools are producing better results, the direct interventions by the Tribal Welfare Department in the field of education has a discouraging effect on the State Education Department, which tends to concentrate on the non-tribal areas assuming that the TW Department is responsible for the promotion of education in the tribal areas.

Non Governmental Organisations and Tribal Development

Advantageous Characteristics of NGOs

The involvement of Non Governmental Organisations (NGOs) in the process of sustainable rural development in countries designated as "developing" all over the world is being considered essential, by some leading NGOs and experts particularly of countries defined as developed and their followers elsewhere. The arguments advanced are that the NGOs are non-bureaucratic, non-hierarchic, and are better in feeling the felt needs at the Micro level, besides being governed by what is called "the articles of faith", i.e., heterogeneity, reaching the poor, participation in decision-making process vs outcome, flexibility, experimentation, institution building and low cost (or no cost on the resource-less Governments due to easy flow of money from the international NGOs/donor agencies).

Traditionally, the scale, scope and influence of NGOs had been limited to the area of relief and welfare. Their increasing interventions in the area of Rural Development and action programmes (resistance movements, etc.,) in the recent years, however, are being seen as creating conflicts and a disquieting situation; not conducive for development or building of a civil society. While there is no doubt that in spite of all the good intentions, there is a limit up to which the "Welfare State" can work in the affairs of human welfare, the role of NGOs in the light of their claim of comparative advantage needs a closer look in a State having Constitutional obligations to build up democratic institutions from the grass-root level and involve them in the process of development.

Importance of NGOs Intenvention

Although the laws provide for-a minimum wage rate, allotment of ceiling surplus and waste land in favour of the landless, prohibition of share cropping system, protection of civil rights by making untouchability and any kind of social discrimination on the ground of birth, a punitive offence and abolition of illegal money lending, etc., —the objectives of these legislations have remained confined to statute books due to lack of awareness among the vulnerable sections about the legislative intentions of the "welfare state" and biased administrative system controlled by vested interests. It is natural that in such a situation, the NGOs charged with emotion and idealism feel for immediate intervention and activism. Aiming at empowerment of the poor, they encounter challenges, including those posed by the dominant power structure, that exists in the village and keeps the vulnerable sections isolated.

Participatory Mobilization and Awareness Generation by NGOs

Some of the indigenous NGOs have performed commendably in organising the weaker sections including tribal communities, land-less, small and marginal farmers besides presenting an alternative approach combining welfare and development together with community-participation, contrary to the regulatory, top down and fragmented approach followed by the government machinery. The increasing demands for minimum wages and social audit of community works executed through contractors or elected bodies are results of participatory mobilisation and awareness generated by some NGOs.

Implementation of Educational Programmes

Education in broad sense of the term is a key and critical input for self-reliant and sustained development. In order to overcome the difficulties in organising and motivating the poor towards small family norms, proper child care, sanitation, functional literacy, etc., the NGOs are providing opportunities for non formal education through night schools to those who did not have access to elementary education during their formative years. To some extent, the night schools opened by NGOs have also given educational opportunity to the children, who help their parents in farm and non-farm activities during the day hours besides supplementing governmental efforts towards universalisation of primary education.

Awareness together with continuing education and participatory processes initiated by some committed grass root organisations, has sensitised and mobilised the rural poor considerably. As awareness alone can not feed the hungry, clothe the naked and heal the sick, some NGOs have initiated income generating schemes taking into account minimum needs of the community in both welfare as well as development sectors. While public health functionaries of government tend to pay occasional visits to villages in connection with family planning and immunisation with the objective of achieving the targets, the NGOs prefer to follow a different path to stimulate the villagers towards preventive health care through improved sanitation and education about the advantages of small family, etc. Some NGOs are engaged in providing safe drinking water and training local artisans for maintenance of tube wells installed by them. Side by side, NGOs are organising the weaker sections of the society, including the women in the rural areas under various income generating activities. There are instances of the rural poor traditionally exploited by money lenders, getting financial assistance from the cooperatives organised for them by NGOs, despite some initial conflicts in the village.

The NGOs have the potential of achieving success in social as well as economic sector, where government machinery may not be very effective and administrative measures may prove inadequate. For example, government regularly allots ceiling surplus and waste land to the landless families, but reality on the ground does not conform fully to what is reported in terms of achievement. The grass root NGOs can organise the allottees of such land and help them in delivery of actual possessions with necessary support from the administration. In addition to providing assistance directly to develop the land, the NGOs can provide free consultancy and advocacy support by bridging the distance between the beneficiaries, banks and government officials, so that the poor really gets what is due to him under the existing delivery system. Such an arrangement facilitates sanction of subsidised loans in favour of allottees for digging of irrigation wells, land development, etc., under the poverty alleviation schemes of the government without approaching any middle man.

By creating awareness about laws and democratic rights through various innovative and conventional methods, the NGOs have been contributing to the building of what may be called a "civil society", in addition to providing opportunities for creativity. No state can succeed in performing such tasks as experience all over the world shows that there is a limit to the positive role of the welfare state in the human welfare. The activities of NGOs can be additive to the governmental efforts to a great extent, if performed hand in had.

NGOs : A Critical Review

A critical review of the activities of NGOs, particularly in the tribal areas and their claims of comparative advantage and competence to develop the capabilities of the poor for self-reliant and sustained development, may however, reveal a gap between the appearance and reality.

The NGOs commonly plead for organising the poor against institution building (Roy S,1989:253-273). While such an approach may have short term effect, its sustainability in a democratic state would be in question, particularly in the event of conflict with the local elected body - a legitimate democratic institution.

The income generating activities of an NGO aim at self-reliance as the continued presence of the NGO cannot be guaranteed and its capacity to assist others will be limited if it continues to service the existing clients (White S.C., 1990:108). The alternative approach for so-called sustainable development claimed by some NGOs has the potential of creating greater dependency, considering the fact that the target group still remains dependent on them, financially and managerially.

Sustainability of development has to be tested in terms of self-manageability, replicability and self-reliance devoid of independence is meaningless. The cooperatives and income generating units started by NGOs in effect are managed by them, and fail to sustain once the NGOs leave the beneficiaries; their development partners and stake holders. In this connection, the saying quoted by Retchil Calder at an OXFAM lecture, so often repeated afterwards, deserves attention- "Give a man a fish and you feed him for today; teach him how to fish and he feeds himself and his family for the rest of his life" (Harris, M., 1988:1).

The whole concept of sustainability and self- reliance, in fact, appears contradictory considering the continuing presence of NGOs in the same areas. The intermediary NGOs of South is dependent on the donors of North. The contradiction becomes clearer when on the one hand the NGOs talk about fostering self-reliant development among the poor and on the other build themselves up as institutions that look set in staying. Indeed, one could find resource rich NGOs indulging in empire building in some places.

No doubt, some village based indigenous NGOs have tried to organise the tribal communities, who are now more assertive than ever before, but, there still remains a wide gap between the appearance of participation and reality. As most of the functionaries of the intermediary NGOs working among rural communities are outsiders, working like any other extension agents of government, the beneficiaries, who are called partners, have hardly any say or participation in the decision making process. Decisions are made keeping in view the mandate of donors and superimposed on the partners.

The NGOs are considered to be in the position of comparative competence and advantage in reaching the poor(Chambers R.,1993:93 and Robinsion M.,1993:28-31). Reaching the poor is not, however, the same as alleviating poverty and empowerment. There are very many processes, relationships and socio-economic structures underlying rural people's poverty: landlessness, low wages, political powerlessness, imperfect markets, adverse micro-economic policy environment and elite controlled policy processes are but a few (Farrington J. and Bebbington A.,1993:92-94). A village based NGO is a marginal player, hardly in a position to address wider scale structural factors that underlie rural poverty. By merely being reached, the poor tends to become dependent on the feeding bottles offered by the intermediary/donor NGOs and encapsulated in a development process, not of their own making. A closer scrutiny of the NGOs' work shows that the rhetoric of capability-building of poor and sustained development through community participation exceeds reality.

The NGOs frequently talk about imparting skill, non-formal education through night schools, extension, motivation and awareness building, etc., among the poor. Despite most of their resources being spent on these activities, they tend to hide the very low literacy rate among the tribal communities even after years of their adequately publicised work and dedicated services for those communities. Indeed, the objective of so-called social audit may not be achieved by momentary mobilisation of masses by spending huge resources made available by donors for such purposes. There is no doubt that the tribals suffer the maximum in any act of displacement as they do not receive adequate compensation for all the land in their cultivating possession, not being legally recorded in their names. Their customary rights which allow them traditional hold over the common property resource, i.e. the community land, is not recognised for awarding compensation at the time of displacement. Although, the rehabilitation packages for setting up industrial projects provide for employment to one of the members of those having lost their land, the only source of sustenance, the tribal communities remain deprived of such benefits due to lack of essential educational qualification. The NGOs leading agitation against the displacement of tribals rarely demand educational facilities for the them, as a part of the rehabilitation package. The displaced tribal families, who have been living in the relative isolation of forests for generations, face a much bigger problem in adjustment on being relocated, elsewhere due to lack of education. As a result, successive generations are subjected to various forms of exploitation. Further, the NGOs do not show the same amount of interest for the formal education as they do for the non-formal education through night school, adult education centres, etc.

In the recent years, the intervention by NGOs, particularly of those having access to foreign funds, in the area of tribal development has become increasingly controversial due to their mystified operations, excessive activism, confrontation with the legitimate grass root democratic bodies and hardly any perceptible impact to show their work making a positive difference while "Challenging the Profession".

Despite working in relatively developed areas, the NGOs seem to have hardly any verifiable evidence for claiming that the beneficiaries in their project villages are better placed than those in the neighbouring villages, in terms of capability development for self-reliant and sustained development. There are not many 'self help groups' with claim making capacity or bargaining power, independent of NGOs. In this regard, the findings of ODI studies about the performance of the intermediary NGOs in India and Bangladesh that they have contributed to the overall improvement of rural poor, though the conditions of the very poorest have not changed much (Robinsion M.A.1991:118 and White S.S., 1991 : 98), is relevant. The overall contribution of NGOs in various field has received universal appreciation in recent years as "the good development work is not insignificant just because it is limited in scale and some might disagree with Clark's statement that maximising impact is the paramount objective of NGOs"(Edward M. and Hulme D. 1993:14).

6

Review of the TSP Approach and Administrative Structure

Features of TSP Approach

The main objectives of the TSP approach have been to narrow the gap between the level of development of tribal and other areas and to improve the quality of life in the tribal communities. The Sub Plan approach envisaged an appropriate legal framework and administrative measures conforming to the objectives and needs of tribal communities. The National Committee on Development of Backward Areas has summed up the key features of the TSP approach as follows:-

"(i) The development of tribal areas has to be conceived in comprehensive terms. Therefore, formal categorisation of various developmental activities, should not be the governing criteria, so far as tribal areas were concerned. The resources for development should be pooled and the priority within these resources should be worked out with reference to the needs of these areas. Problem solving approach with clear objective should be adopted making the system flexible.

(ii) Tribal area development has to be an integral part of the total development of the State and the Nation. Major thrust of their development has to be provided by various sectoral authorities themselves.

(iii) The special responsibility of the Union Government in terms of the Constitutional provisions was also spelt out. Each Ministry is responsible for development of these areas in relation to its functional jurisdiction. They should review the tribal situation and provide necessary investment for their speedy development.

(iv) Another basic premise in tribal development is the recognition of the fact that the socio-economic situation may require a specific answer. The basic unit of planning and implementation, which should be homogeneous and viable was defined as Integrated Tribal Development Project. The Sub Plan should be built from below and represent an organic build up of project planning.

(v) The primitive tribal communities should be identified and special programmes with adequate flexibility should be built up for them.

(vi) The administration system for tribal areas should be simple and over-specialisation discouraged so that the system was within the comprehension of the community which it was supposed to serve. Adequate administrative and financial power should be delegated and responsibility at each level should be specific" (RDTA, 1981:15-16).

Limitations of TSP Approach

The conceptual frame of the TSP approach has been sound and need-based. However, the actual planning and implementation differed from the theoretical frame due to deviations at various levels. The approach was conceived centrally but responsibility to implement it was left to the States without providing adequate funds, effective monitoring mechanism and specific directions. The Constitutional provisions for a flexible and accountable administrative set up for planning and implementation of tribal development with local participation, got diluted at various levels starting from the top. The Central Ministries never cared to act upon the guidelines prescribed for them. Neither sufficient funds were provided by the Union Government for strengthening of administration under the mandatory provisions of Article 275 of the Constitution.

Functioning of TSP

The TSP approach proposes functional integration among various programmes through a single administrative unit at the ITDP level. All the departments are required to intimate the quantum of funds likely to be allotted under different schemes to the Project Administrators of ITDPs for preparation of the Action Plan with the approval of the Project Level Committee(PLC), consisting of people's representatives and district level officers of line departments. In practice, the functional integration rarely takes place. The ITDPs/ITDAs hardly find themselves in a position of preparing need based Action Plans keeping in view the quantification of funds by different line departments for schemes relating to their sectors.

The quantification in reality is notional, as if to observe the formality of the plan exercise. The ITDPs remain ineffective as the planning process continues to be a "top-down" process. The role of ITDPs/ITDAs has been diluted and changed from the planning and coordinating bodies to the executing agencies. A portion of the Special Central Assistance is released to them for the implementation of family oriented income generating schemes. The TSP document, which is expected to be an integrated plan of action at the State level becomes a routine formal exercise.

The Project Level Committee (PLC) of ITDP is the supreme body for formulation and implementation of its plan. The jurisdiction of the Project covers a number of blocks. Each block is administered by an elective body known as Panchayat Samiti. As an elective body, the Samiti expects the final say in the formulation of the block plan. Therefore, a certain amount of conflict arises between the PLC and Panchayat Samity. Both ITDPs and Panchayat Samities are controlled by two different departments at the district and State level. Again, the Panchyat Samiti which eventually implements the tribal development projects does not take enough interest as its own schemes are not accepted by the PLC.

ITDAs and DRDAs

Reasons for Ineffectiveness

Another dimension that complicates the situation is the establishment of District Rural Development Agencies (DRDAs) at the district level. A large number of parallel poverty alleviation projects are being implemented by the DRDAs in Sub Plan districts at the same time. Most of the schemes under implementation by ITDPs and DRDAs are identical, and have common beneficiaries. Instead of pooling resources together for drawing integrated action plans, both the agencies tend to work parallel to each other and in isolation. The multiplicity and complexity of administrative machinery helps only in confusing the innocent tribals. Over-administration does more harm than good to them due to their inability to grasp the differentiations of administrative structures.

The Scheduled Areas and Scheduled Tribes Commission (Dhevar Commission) had suggested that the blocks with above 50 per cent to tribal population should form part of the Scheduled Area. Compactness of the area along with the concentration of the tribal population was the foundation stone of the TSP approach conceived during the Fifth Five Year Plan. The ITDP which took agency form in the name of ITDA with the passage of time was required to be the basic structure for preparation, supervision and monitoring of all the plans and programmes in the Scheduled Area. But this concept could not take a concrete shape due to parallel formation of District Rural Development Agency (DRDA) in TSP districts. The DRDA was made the main instrument for designing and supervising all the rural developmental projects and poverty alleviation schemes through the Blocks, Panchayat Raj Institutions and other line departments. The ITDA lost whatever little hold it had on the Blocks having concentration of tribal population. In a complete role reversal, it started implementing projects from the additive allocations received directly under the Special Central Assistance. The basic objective behind the constitution the ITDA got defeated. This institutional dichotomy not only resulted in the diffusion of accountability for the uplift of tribals and development of scheduled area but also confused the simple minded single command driven tribal communities required to be serviced under one umbrella. The Project Level Committees of ITDP/ITDA did not have any control over the DRDA and coordination without some amount of control was a remote possibility. Instead of pooling resources together, both the agencies ie. the ITDA and the DRDA started doing the same work directly or through Blocks and other line departments. In course of time, the ITDAs were further relegated to the background. The line departments preferred to access funds from the DRDAs which received more funds for implementing the poverty alleviation schemes and development of rural infrastructure. The resources of DRDA were spent more for the benefits of non-tribals living in the scheduled areas under the popular impression that the ITDA were doing enough for development of tribal communities.

Multiplicity of Administration

The Tribal Sub-plan approach envisaged implementation of welfare schemes, programmes for economic uplift of tribals and protective measures under one umbrella keeping in view the needs and difficulties of tribal communities who were not aware of the finer specialization in different branches of administration. The constitution of PLC/ITDA was to facilitate drafting of plans and programmes according to the felt needs of tribals in the sub plan areas by pooling resources to be made available by different departments and implement them in a cohesive and coordinated manner under a single line administration. In reality, the administrative network got increasingly multiplied in the Sub-plan areas, like elsewhere, with hardly any attempts to establish functional integration among different branches of administration. The recommendations made by Maheshwar Dayal Committee for a single line administration were not implemented except on a limited scale in the tribal sub plan areas of Andhra Pradesh.

The Regional Administrative Bodies, wherever constituted, failed to discharge their responsibilities with effectiveness. The plan funds meant for the sub plan areas were required to be allocated ITDA wise in desegregated form through the Regional Development Bodies to enable them to do effective planning, monitoring and implementation of schemes in the scheduled areas. But this conceptual framework was not translated into real practice. The line departments continued to release funds to their district level heads following the earlier practices, as usual.

The Tribes Advisory Councils (TACs) were constituted in different States under 5th Schedule of the Constitution. They were expected to advise in matters relating to the overall development of tribals. However, with the passage of time, TACs failed to make the desired impact. The Governors of States having scheduled areas rarely exercised their constitutional authority and obligations to improve the levels of administration in the scheduled areas. The annual report on the administration of scheduled areas to be submitted to the President regularly, became a perfunctory exercise without being observed with regularity.

There is no integration between the two branches of administration dealing with the protection and regulatory measures and developmental programmes, although both these branches of the administrative structure are mutually reinforcing and interdependent in the context of tribal development.

Again, there is multiplicity of organisations depending upon their specialisations under the two branches of administration. The tribal farmer can not procure seeds and fertilizer from a single window. For a docile tribal, these finer specializations of administration are confusing and attempts at getting any help lead to futility or harassment. A very simplistic unitary administrative organisation providing a package of help in time is most suitable to the tribal situation. The integrated functional approach has multiple advantages. It provides better services with less personnel, in addition to cutting across the narrow sense of departmentalism and cutting down heavy overhead expenditure. Sadly, on the top of the continuing problem of coordination, postings to the tribal areas are viewed as measures of punishment, which generate complaint psychology and stand in the way of enthusiastic and efficient work.

Suggestions for Successful Implementation

The successful implementation of development programmes depends on the involvement of the beneficiaries. The general tendency in the administration at times is to blame the tribals for the failures of the schemes instead of involving them in the process of planning and implementation. Intimate relationship and closer interaction between the administrative staff and tribals is absolutely necessary. The tribal people can be involved in project formulation and implementation by working through their traditional political system. Instead of superimposing new organisations, it is desirable to strengthen the much stronger traditional village organisations/institutions by assigning progressively participatory roles to them.

Government of India in the Ministry of Home affairs, constituted a Study Group under the chairmanship of Maheshwar Prasad, in 1978 to examine the question of conditions in the tribal areas and to give suggestions for evolving a right type of personnel policy. Some important recommendations in the "Report of the Study Group on Administrative Arrangements and Personnel Policies" are: Integration of administrative units in the area of Integrated Tribal Development Projects leading to a rational command, right from the Tribal Commissioner to the project administrator of an ITDP; the administrative structure at the block level should become an integral part of the chain and the BDO should be brought under the control and supervision of the project administrator; the staffing pattern of the Block should be strengthened; in the area of ITDP, there should be one organisation called upon to perform developmental functions replacing multiplicity of agencies; adequate tribal representations should be secured in the spheres of planning and implementation and for expression of their point of view; adequate administrative and financial delegation should be made in favour of the Project Administrators of the ITDPs; adequate role in budgeting, sanction, diversions, etc. for TSP area should vest in the Tribal Development department; adequate funds should be set apart for educational and health institutions and communications for creation of physical facilities in tribal areas; suitable cadres for persons committed to work in the difficult tribal areas be built up; acquisition of good knowledge of a tribal dialect within a prescribed period should be made a condition for appointment in the cadre of field functionaries; both, monetary and non-monetary incentives should be given to the personnel in recognition of their services in tribal areas; instruments of proper evaluation and monitoring should be evolved in the States and Centre and utilized fully.

Non-adherence of the Financial Framework under the TSP Approach

The TSP approach envisaged earmarking of funds by each Department in the State and Central Ministries for schemes directly benefiting tribal communities. In reality, neither the Central Ministries nor the State Departments followed this frame work with seriousness. The earmarking of funds proportionate to the tribal population became an annual budgetary exercise. Indeed, funds earmarked under the divisible sectors were always inadequate and diverted, quite frequently, other areas on one ground or other. The visible higher allocations for non-divisible sectors like industrial-mining and multipurpose irrigation projects, etc. in the TSP areas had the actual beneficiaries mostly in the non-tribal areas, elsewhere. Article 275 of the Constitution provided for release of grant from the Consolidated Fund of India to meet the cost of such schemes of developments as may be undertaken by the States with the approval of the Government of India. These schemes are meant for the purpose of promoting the welfare of Scheduled Tribes in that State or raising the level of administration of scheduled areas therein to that of the administration of the rest of the areas of that State. Ironically, the limited funds released under this mandatory Constitutional provision were rarely spent for the specified purpose by most of the States. Although, the line Departments at the State level were required to communicate their desegregated budgetary provisions to the ITDAs for integrated planning, it did not happen in practice. The ITDAs started working like executing agencies, leaving their role of policy planning and supervisory bodies for implementation of schemes in the Sub-plan areas. They remained satisfied by spending the limited amount of the Special Central Assistance, which according to the financial framework of the TSP Approach was just an additive to the State plan.

Extension of Panchayat Provisions to the Scheduled Areas

The Panchayat Raj Institutions were accorded constitutional status through the 73rd Constitutional Amendment in 1992. The provisions of the Panchayats have been extended to the scheduled areas through an Act passed by Parliament in 1996. The extension of Panchayats to the scheduled areas do not go hand in hand with the provisions of the 5th Schedule of the Constitution. The Act under reference seeks to super impose Panchayat Raj bodies on the scheduled areas ignoring the prevailing environment and traditional bodies which are more effective at the grassroots level. This Act also seeks to reserve above 50 per cent seats of Panchayat at all levels in addition to heading the Scheduled Tribes in the scheduled areas ignoring that in large number of Blocks in the scheduled areas, tribal communities do not account for the majority of population. There are many Blocks in scheduled areas of different States with tribal population ranging from 6.5 to 49 per cent and a mechanical approach in reservation presuming scheduled areas to be coterminus with the tribal majority areas may further isolate the tribal communities by creating social conflicts. Despite the Commission on Scheduled Areas and Scheduled Tribes (Dhebar Commission) recommending blocks having more than 50 per cent tribal population only to be included in the scheduled area, the Constitution order 1950 specifying the scheduled areas with many non-tribal majority Blocks has not been amended, suitably.

The Commissioner for Scheduled Caste and Scheduled Tribes, in his 29th report (1989: 371-372), has made critical observations for what has been noted by him as violation of safeguards for tribals in the Constitution under fifth and sixth schedules; for the administration of the scheduled areas. The new administrative set up and laws according to the report, have been extended in a routine fashion in the tribal areas, ignoring the unwritten laws, conventions and age-old traditions and institutions of tribals. Instead of recognising the existing local system, a new scheme of Panchayat(elected village council) has been introduced in tribal areas. While the new organisation superimposed has not succeeded, the traditional systems are becoming increasingly weaker to the disadvantage of tribals.

The Governors of States having scheduled areas have been given vast powers under the fifth schedule of the Constitution for making suitable changes in the administration of the scheduled areas, keeping the customs and traditional set-up of tribals in view. But, there has hardly been any conscious attempt on their part to issue directives to follow the Constitutional provisions in respect of administering the scheduled areas by developing a pragmatic administrative set-up conforming to the needs and understanding of tribals.

7

Conclusions and Recommendations

Development Administration in a Welfare State has been considered an important instrument to expedite the process of change through planned development and positive actions. The process of development is always incomplete and relative. The main aim of development is to increase the per capita income, to raise the standards of living of the people and to secure justice, freedom, equality and security for them in the society. The total well-being is measured in terms of the facilities and services that are available.

In tune with the objectives and paradigms of development and constructive role of the Welfare State, the Five Year Plans were launched in India after independence with some special priorities to eradicate different handicaps and disabilities of the under-privileged groups such as scheduled tribes. Distinctive Constitutional provisions envisaged in keeping with the spirit of time, adequate provisions for continuous readjustments amongst various elements. The focus shifted from the earlier "isolationist" approach to "assimilation" with necessary safeguards for transitional period so that their interests were not adversely affected.

The successive plan efforts have been stepped forward to translate the Constitutional goals. The Fifth Five Year Plan (1974-79) may be regarded as a watershed in the history of tribal development in the country, which gave birth to the concept of TSP approach. The sixth, seventh and Five Year Plans gave further boost to it by simultaneously launching a large number of family oriented income generating schemes and infrastructure development projects. The fact that 1.26 million tribal families were assisted under different poverty alleviation schemes out of the total tribal population of 5.9 millions in Orissa state alone, during the 6th and 7th plan period (TSP Orissa, 1992-98:55), indicates the serious concern of the State towards tribal development on a preferential footing. However, it would be far from reality to say that all the tribal communities in the country have reached the level of development, comparable with the non-tribals.

Recommendation

A critical analysis of the Tribal Development Administration as mentioned in this book reveals that the pace of progress in the process of change in tribal areas and among tribals has not been up to the expectation and tribals have not been able to share the fruits of development equally and uniformly due to historical reasons, and because of defects and dilutions in the legal as well as developmental administration. Some corrective measures for further refinement in the strategy of tribal development are being suggested as follows :

Land Matters

The tribal economy has remained centred around land and land based resources. Even today, land continues to be the mainstay of more than 90 per cent of the tribal population. It should therefore be the most important task to remove the defects of land administration by incorporating suitable changes in relevant laws and rules. The survey and settlement operations in some States are carried out through cadastral and plain table techniques, which do not make it possible to measure the land beyond 10 degree slope, even if the land is under the cultivating possession of the tribal farmers for generations. The technical rules governing the settlement operation should therefore be changed.

As a result of non-recognition of communal rights, the embedded rights of tribals also fail to be recorded. Among some of the tribes, there are individual rights subsumed within community control, management and ownership. The separation of individual from the community in matters of property relations concerning land has been a Colonial hand-over, which continues to affect the tribals even today. The general laws disallowing community ownership over land, therefore should not be applied to all the tribal communities generally. Tribal community organisations may be recognised as privileged royats (land holders) in the same manner as the Deities and Religious Trusts owning land without being governed by the land ceiling laws.

Acquisition of tribal land by government for "public purpose" under various land acquisition laws at times drives the tribal to the extreme situation of distress. All the displaced families do not get compensation proportionate to their land acquired, simply because the community control over the land and individual control over 10 degree slope are not taken into account. Besides, due to lower priority to the survey operations to the tribal areas, the realities are not reflected in the records of right. It is therefore necessary to expedite the process of survey operations in tribal areas and incorporate suitable changes in land acquisition laws and rules.

In addition to recognising the symbiotic relations between forests and tribals, all the forest land under the cultivating possession of tribals should be recorded in their favour without any pre-condition. In the management of forests, age-old partnership of tribals with forests should not be discarded. The provisions of the forest conservation laws, which do not recognise traditional rights of tribals, should be withheld by Governors in scheduled areas exercising powers under the Fifth Schedule of the Constitution.

Development of Communication System

Robert Chambers (1983: 13-21) writes about the various biases which impede outsider's contact with rural poverty. He strongly criticises the visiting experts of what he calls "rural development tourism", who are affected by the "road side bias". To prove his point, he refers to the remote tribal districts of central India, not receiving enough "rural development tourists"! Unfortunately, he loses sight of the fact that the only way to break the bias is by development of appropriate communication network.

Socio-economic development of tribals and scheduled areas has been slow due to infrastructural weaknesses. The results of family oriented poverty alleviation schemes have not been commensurate with the financial investment and physical efforts because of lack of forward and backward linkages. The field functionaries of key development departments do not respond to their postings to the remote tribal areas lacking basic amenities, which weakens the delivery system at the cutting edge of administration. The successful implementation of social welfare schemes, essential services and regulatory administration is dependent upon the existence of effective communication system. Priorities should therefore be given to the development of a communication system with greater emphasis on the area development approach.

Earmarking of funds for development of infrastructure in the TSP area should be done considering the existing backwardness and geographical area, and not on the basis of percentage of the tribal population. Similarly, instead of considering the total population of a revenue village as a unit for construction of roads under the Minimum Needs Programmes, the population in a cluster of hamlets should be the criteria of consideration as the tribals live in thinly populated scattered villages.

Poverty Alleviation Schemes

One of the reasons of large-scale indebtedness of tribals is the indiscriminate implementation of non-viable loan linked schemes and consequential default in repayment. Emphasis should therefore be laid on land based schemes like land development, smaller irrigation projects, soil and water conservation measures. Tribal regions are the origins of large number of perennial and semi perennial streams on which low cost environment friendly irrigation systems can be developed for durable gains of tribals. Fortunately, despite problems of land alienation, tribals at large are not affected by landlessness. Development of land and creation of irrigation potential may improve the quality of their cultivable land.

Education

The basic problem of tribal communities is how to negotiate the period of change when all of a sudden, they come in contact with a new system, without losing the command over their resources. It therefore, follows that highest priority should be given to education in a comprehensive sense of the term so that the community is enabled to stand on its own through building its inner strength and understanding intricacies of the new systems. The investment in education should be much more and residential institutions should be opened in tribal areas to compensate the lack of parental awareness towards education among the tribals.

Administrative Reforms

The successful implementation of the planning process depends upon the quality of manpower responsible for handling the plans and programmes. Unfortunately, tribal areas have been treated as sanctuaries for negligent functionaries, who are shunted there as a measure of punishment. It may not be irrelevant to restate that Government functionaries with unimpeachable track-records, who are willing to work in tribal areas should only be posted to serve the tribals with adequate delegation of administrative and financial powers and specific responsibilities. They should be compensated by monetary and other incentives. As far as possible, officers belonging to tribal communities should be associated in the process of planning and implementation of the schemes.

Multiplicity of administration has invariably resulted in the diffusion of accountability in addition to confusing the simple minded tribals. The concept of Single Line Administration for both-protective as well as developmental works, should be introduced in tribal areas.

Lastly, the effective functioning of democratic institutions pre-supposes a certain degree of awareness, education and moral standards. With morality at a discount among the public functionaries and a negligible level of education and awareness of the modern democratic institutions among the tribal communities, superimposition of the so-called democratic institutions does more harm than good. It would therefore be desirable to recognise the much stronger traditional bodies of tribal communities and associate them in the planning and implementation of the developmental projects till the demand for democratisation of public institutions comes from the tribals themselves.

PART-II
DISTRICTWISE DISTRIBUTION OF SCHEDULED TRIBES POPULATION BY SEX

BALANGIR
(Undivided)

District	*Total/ Rural/ Urban*	*Population*		
		Total	*Males*	*Females*
1	*2*	*3*	*4*	*5*
All Scheduled Tribes				
	Total	3,16,797	1,57,971	1,58,826
	Rural	3,08,398	1,53,673	1,54,725
	Urban	8,399	4,298	4,101
1. Bagata				
	Total	40	18	22
	Rural	40	18	22
2. Baiga				
	Total	88	11	77
	Rural	88	11	77
3. Banjara, Banjari				
	Total	577	278	299
	Rural	541	273	268
	Urban	36	5	31
4. Bathudi				
	Total	34	6	28
	Rural	20	1	19
	Urban	14	5	9
5. Bhuiya, Bhuyan				
	Total	67	30	37
	Rural	19	7	12
	Urban	48	23	25

6. Bhumij				
	Total	12	12	0
	Rural	2	2	0
	Urban	10	10	0
7. Bhunjia				
	Total	72	22	50
	Rural	72	22	50
8. Binjhal				
	Total	37,242	18,585	18,657
	Rural	37,094	18,493	18,601
	Urban	148	92	56
9. Binjhia, Binjhoa				
	Total	162	79	83
	Rural	162	79	83
10. Birhor				
	Total	99	63	36
	Rural	90	54	36
	Urban	9	9	0
11. Bondo Poraja				
	Total	197	100	97
	Rural	179	100	79
	Urban	18	0	18
12. Chenchu				
	Total	2	0	2
	Rural	2	0	2
13. Dal				
	Total	14,674	7,173	7,501
	Rural	14,640	7,150	7,490
	Urban	34	23	11
14. Desua Bhumij				
	Total	210	136	74
	Rural	208	134	74
	Urban	2	2	0

15. Dharua				
	Total	263	191	72
	Rural	259	187	72
	Urban	4	4	0
16. Didayi				
	Total	33	33	0
	Rural	33	33	0
17. Gadaba				
	Total	42	32	10
	Rural	42	32	10
18. Gandia				
	Total	53	15	38
	Rural	49	13	36
	Urban	4	2	2
19. Ghara				
	Total	256	120	136
	Rural	256	120	136
20. Gond, Gondo				
	Total	93,331	46,718	46,613
	Rural	92,259	46,207	46,052
	Urban	1,072	511	561
21. Ho				
	Total	54	23	31
	Rural	45	14	31
	Urban	9	9	0
22. Holva				
	Total	14	11	3
	Rural	14	11	3
23. Jatapu				
	Total	41	12	29
	Rural	40	11	29
	Urban	1	1	0

24. Juang

	Total	12	12	0
	Rural	12	12	0

25. Kandha Gauda

	Total	633	325	308
	Rural	605	298	307
	Urban	28	27	1

26. Kawar

	Total	128	60	68
	Rural	120	54	66
	Urban	8	6	2

27. Kharia, Kharian

	Total	3,434	1,614	1,820
	Rural	3,110	1,468	1,642
	Urban	324	146	178

28. Kharwar

	Total	26	11	15
	Rural	16	1	15
	Urban	10	10	0

29. Khond, Kond, Kandha, Nanguli Kandha, Sitha Kandha

	Total	83,577	41,509	42,068
	Rural	81,406	40,420	40,986
	Urban	2,171	1,089	1,082

30. Kisan

	Total	535	317	218
	Rural	507	300	207
	Urban	28	17	11

31. Kolah Loharas, Kol Loharas

	Total	583	280	303
	Rural	519	268	251
	Urban	64	12	52

32. Kolha	Total	2,205	1,057	1,148
	Rural	2,143	1,024	1,119
	Urban	62	33	29
33. Koli, Malhar	Total	325	156	169
	Rural	267	117	150
	Urban	58	39	19
34. Kondadora	Total	279	126	153
	Rural	242	108	134
	Urban	37	18	19
35. Kora	Total	620	353	267
	Rural	612	345	267
	Urban	8	8	0
36. Korua	Total	78	26	52
	Rural	78	26	52
37. Kotia	Total	91	48	43
	Rural	82	39	43
	Urban	9	9	0
38. Koya	Total	30	16	14
	Rural	29	16	13
	Urban	1	0	1
39. Kulis	Total	1,094	492	602
	Rural	923	413	510
	Urban	171	79	92

40. Lodha				
	Total	38	18	20
	Rural	17	6	11
	Urban	21	12	9
41. Madia				
	Total	68	0	68
	Rural	68	0	68
42. Mahali				
	Total	193	91	102
	Rural	163	83	80
	Urban	30	8	22
43. Mankidi				
	Total	1	0	1
	Rural	1	0	1
44. Mankirdia				
	Total	126	33	93
	Rural	126	33	93
45. Matya				
	Total	36	21	15
	Rural	36	21	15
46. Mirdhas				
	Total	6,891	3,568	3,323
	Rural	6,650	3,430	3,220
	Urban	241	138	103
47. Munda, Munda Lohara, Munda Mahalis				
	Total	3,768	1,825	1,943
	Rural	3,165	1,512	1,653
	Urban	603	313	290
48. Mundari				
	Total	95	43	52
	Rural	93	41	52
	Urban	2	2	0

49. Omanatya				
	Total	63	11	52
	Rural	63	11	52
50. Oraon				
	Total	207	104	103
	Rural	158	67	91
	Urban	49	37	12
51. Parenga				
	Total	354	190	164
	Rural	331	167	164
	Urban	23	23	0
52. Paroja				
	Total	128	64	64
	Rural	118	63	55
	Urban	10	1	9
53. Pentia				
	Total	27	27	0
	Rural	20	20	0
	Urban	7	7	0
54. Rajuar				
	Total	23	2	21
	Rural	23	2	21
55. Santal				
	Total	127	75	52
	Rural	78	48	30
	Urban	49	27	22
56. Saora, Savar, Saura, Sahara				
	Total	49,023	24,903	24,120
	Rural	47,333	24,048	23,285
	Urban	1,690	855	835
57. Shabar, Lodha				
	Total	14,243	6,864	7,379
	Rural	12,960	6,181	6,779
	Urban	1,283	683	600

58. Sounti				
	Total	79	33	46
	Rural	77	31	46
	Urban	2	2	0
59. Tharua				
	Total	93	28	65
	Rural	93	28	65
60. Unclassified				
	Total	1	1	0
	Urban	1	1	0

Note: 1. All Scheduled Tribes includes figures for 'unclassified'.
2. Tribes having nil return are not shown.

BALESHWAR
(Undivided)

District	*Total/ Rural/ Urban*	*Population*		
		Total	*Males*	*Females*
1	*2*	*3*	*4*	*5*
All Scheduled Tribes				
	Total	1,97,992	1,00,609	97,383
	Rural	1,81,889	92,185	89,704
	Urban	16,103	8,424	7,679
1. Bagata				
	Total	107	58	49
	Rural	107	58	49
2. Baiga				
	Total	31	11	20
	Rural	31	11	20
3. Banjara, Banjari				
	Total	40	18	22
	Rural	40	18	22
4. Bathudi				
	Total	12,659	6,589	6,070
	Rural	12,533	6,508	6,025
	Urban	126	81	45
5. Bhottada, Dhotada				
	Total	95	37	58
	Rural	86	29	57
	Urban	9	8	1

6. Bhuiya, Bhuyan				
	Total	1,268	712	556
	Rural	1,160	628	532
	Urban	108	84	24
7. Bhumia				
	Total	93	20	73
	Rural	91	18	73
	Urban	2	2	0
8. Bhumij				
	Total	47,044	24,179	22,865
	Rural	43,647	22,307	21,340
	Urban	3,397	1,872	1,525
9. Bhunjia				
	Total	111	61	50
	Rural	97	57	40
	Urban	14	4	10
10. Binjhal				
	Total	136	52	84
	Rural	136	52	84
11. Binjhia, Binjhoa				
	Total	57	20	37
	Rural	57	20	37
12. Birhor				
	Total	8	8	0
	Rural	8	8	0
13. Bondo Poraja				
	Total	1	0	1
	Rural	1	0	1
1[illegible]. Chenchu				
	Total	3	3	0
	Urban	3	3	0

15. Dal				
	Total	420	131	289
	Rural	410	131	279
	Urban	10	0	10
16. Desua Bhumij				
	Total	331	165	166
	Rural	293	154	139
	Urban	38	11	27
17. Dharua				
	Total	20	7	13
	Rural	20	7	13
18. Didayi				
	Total	10	0	10
	Rural	10	0	10
19. Gadaba				
	Total	36	10	26
	Rural	36	10	26
20. Gandia				
	Total	40	33	7
	Rural	40	33	7
21. Ghara				
	Total	18	10	8
	Rural	18	10	8
22. Gond, Gondo				
	Total	1,287	549	738
	Rural	1,204	492	712
	Urban	83	57	26
23. Ho				
	Total	288	121	167
	Rural	283	116	167
	Urban	5	5	0

24. Holva				
	Total	29	19	10
	Rural	29	19	10
25. Jatapu				
	Total	160	61	99
	Rural	133	38	95
	Urban	27	23	4
26. Juang				
	Total	22	10	12
	Rural	21	9	12
	Urban	1	1	0
27. Kandha Gauda				
	Total	197	76	121
	Rural	184	73	111
	Urban	13	3	10
28. Kawar				
	Total	16	5	11
	Rural	15	4	11
	Urban	1	1	0
29. Kharia, Kharian				
	Total	931	461	470
	Rural	922	452	470
	Urban	9	9	0
30. Kharwar				
	Total	35	33	2
	Rural	35	33	2
31. Khond, Kond, Kandha, Nanguli Kandha, Sitha Kandha				
	Total	301	114	187
	Rural	243	111	132
	Urban	58	3	55
32. Kisan				
	Total	77	23	54
	Rural	65	22	43
	Urban	12	1	11

33. Kol

	Total	349	214	135
	Rural	340	212	128
	Urban	9	2	7

34. Kolah Loharas, Kol Loharas

	Total	300	125	175
	Rural	290	125	165
	Urban	10	0	10

35. Kolha

	Total	31,917	16,050	15,867
	Rural	30,917	15,550	15,367
	Urban	1,000	500	500

36. Koli, Malhar

	Total	57	34	23
	Rural	56	33	23
	Urban	1	1	0

37. Kondadora

	Total	22	22	0
	Rural	22	22	0

38. Kora

	Total	1,080	588	492
	Rural	945	521	424
	Urban	135	67	68

39. Korua

	Total	203	69	134
	Rural	174	67	107
	Urban	29	2	27

40. Kotia

	Total	20	12	8
	Rural	20	12	8

41. Koya

	Total	2	2	0
	Rural	2	2	0

42. Kulis				
	Total	28	1	27
	Rural	28	1	27
43. Lodha				
	Total	2	2	0
	Rural	2	2	0
44. Madia				
	Total	196	90	106
	Rural	196	90	106
45. Mahali				
	Total	224	105	119
	Rural	214	95	119
	Urban	10	10	0
46. Mankidi				
	Total	146	53	93
	Rural	146	53	93
47. Mankirdia				
	Total	8	7	1
	Rural	8	7	1
48. Matya				
	Total	651	340	311
	Rural	637	336	301
	Urban	14	4	10
49. Mirdhas				
	Total	147	105	42
	Rural	143	102	41
	Urban	4	3	1
50. Munda, Munda Lohara, Munda Mahalis				
	Total	7,745	3,673	4,072
	Rural	6,654	3,092	3,562
	Urban	1,091	581	510

51. Mundari				
	Total	1,205	531	674
	Rural	736	338	398
	Urban	469	193	276
52. Omanatya				
	Total	80	56	24
	Rural	47	32	15
	Urban	33	24	9
53. Oraon				
	Total	1,508	901	607
	Rural	1,459	863	596
	Urban	49	38	11
54. Parenga				
	Total	32	12	20
	Rural	32	12	20
55. Paroja				
	Total	67	54	13
	Rural	59	46	13
	Urban	8	8	0
56. Pentia				
	Total	95	58	37
	Rural	93	58	35
	Urban	2	0	2
57. Rajuar				
	Total	166	81	85
	Rural	56	34	22
	Urban	110	47	63
58. Santal				
	Total	72,844	37,602	35,242
	Rural	64,734	33,395	31,339
	Urban	8,110	4,207	3,903

59. Saora, Savar, Saura, Sahara				
	Total	2,344	1,090	1,254
	Rural	2,234	1,051	1,183
	Urban	110	39	71
60. Shabar, Lodha				
	Total	3,337	1,632	1,705
	Rural	3,179	1,560	1,619
	Urban	158	72	86
61. Sounti				
	Total	1,891	872	1,019
	Rural	1,891	872	1,019
62. Tharua				
	Total	148	76	72
	Rural	126	67	59
	Urban	22	9	13
63. Unclassified				
	Total	5,307	2,556	2,751
	Rural	4,494	2,107	2,387
	Urban	813	449	364

Note: 1. All Scheduled Tribes includes figures for 'unclassified'.
2. Tribes having nil return are not shown.

CUTTACK
(Undivided)

District	*Total/ Rural/ Urban*	*Population*		
		Total	*Males*	*Females*
1	*2*	*3*	*4*	*5*
All Scheduled Tribes				
	Total	1,82,188	93,219	88,969
	Rural	1,67,989	85,443	82,546
	Urban	14,199	7,776	6,423
1. Bagata				
	Total	41	41	0
	Rural	13	13	0
	Urban	28	28	0
2. Baiga				
	Total	58	32	26
	Rural	54	30	24
	Urban	4	2	2
3. Banjara, Banjari				
	Total	2	1	1
	Rural	2	1	1
4. Bathudi				
	Total	966	520	446
	Rural	878	454	424
	Urban	88	66	22
5. Bhottada, Dhotada				
	Total	28	2	26
	Rural	20	0	20
	Urban	8	2	6

6. Bhuiya, Bhuyan				
	Total	695	371	324
	Rural	606	308	298
	Urban	89	63	26
7. Bhumia				
	Total	16	15	1
	Rural	12	12	0
	Urban	4	3	1
8. Bhumij				
	Total	5,257	2,661	2,596
	Rural	4,864	2,422	2,442
	Urban	393	239	154
9. Bhunjia				
	Total	72	49	23
	Rural	40	27	13
	Urban	32	22	10
10. Binjhal				
	Total	31	24	7
	Rural	28	21	7
	Urban	3	3	0
11. Binjhia, Binjhoa				
	Total.	1	0	1
	Rural	1	0	1
12. Birhor				
	Total	34	15	19
	Rural	14	12	2
	Urban	20	3	17
13. Chenchu				
	Total	2	2	0
	Rural	1	1	0
	Urban	1	1	0

14. Dal				
	Total	14	13	1
	Rural	14	13	1
15. Desua Bhumij				
	Total	206	118	88
	Rural	95	58	37
	Urban	111	60	51
16. Dharua				
	Total	352	179	173
	Rural	351	179	172
	Urban	1	0	1
17. Didayi				
	Total	5	3	2
	Rural	5	3	2
18. Gadaba				
	Total	34	8	26
	Rural	12	0	12
	Urban	22	8	14
19. Gandia				
	Total	44	32	12
	Rural	44	32	12
20. Ghara				
	Total	108	44	64
	Rural	98	43	55
	Urban	10	1	9
21. Gond, Gondo				
	Total	665	326	339
	Rural	545	239	306
	Urban	120	87	33
22. Ho				
	Total	2,072	1,005	1,067
	Rural	1,832	874	958
	Urban	240	131	109

23. Holva				
	Total	1	1	0
	Rural	1	1	0
24. Jatapu				
	Total	12	3	9
	Rural	3	3	0
	Urban	9	0	9
25. Juang				
	Total	783	399	384
	Rural	779	395	384
	Urban	4	4	0
26. Kandha Gauda				
	Total	391	239	152
	Rural	387	235	152
	Urban	4	4	0
27. Kawar				
	Total	135	58	77
	Rural	124	57	67
	Urban	11	1	10
28. Kharia, Kharian				
	Total	455	222	233
	Rural	388	168	220
	Urban	67	54	13
29. Kharwar				
	Total	1,717	787	930
	Rural	1,714	784	930
	Urban	3	3	0
30. Khond, Kond, Kandha, Nanguli Kandha, Sitha Kandha				
	Total	6,160	3,518	2,642
	Rural	5,761	3,302	2,459
	Urban	399	216	183

31. Kisan				
	Total	122	48	74
	Rural	83	24	59
	Urban	39	24	15
32. Kol				
	Total	989	531	458
	Rural	952	512	440
	Urban	37	19	18
33. Kolah Loharas, Kol Loharas				
	Total	865	320	545
	Rural	842	310	532
	Urban	23	10	13
34. Kolha				
	Total	14,793	7,344	7,449
	Rural	13,844	6,832	7,012
	Urban	949	512	437
35. Koli, Malhar				
	Total	664	340	324
	Rural	615	302	313
	Urban	49	38	11
36. Kondadora				
	Total	14	3	11
	Rural	5	2	3
	Urban	9	1	8
37. Kora				
	Total	90	52	38
	Rural	46	44	2
	Urban	44	8	36
38. Korua				
	Total	46	13	33
	Rural	37	12	25
	Urban	9	1	8

39. Kotia				
	Total	22	18	4
	Rural	21	17	4
	Urban	1	1	0
40. Koya				
	Total	7	5	2
	Rural	7	5	2
41. Kulis				
	Total	36	27	9
	Rural	36	27	9
42. Lodha				
	Total	1,775	1,141	634
	Rural	1,771	1,137	634
	Urban	4	4	0
43. Madia				
	Total	48	31	17
	Rural	46	29	17
	Urban	2	2	0
44. Mahali				
	Total	58	34	24
	Rural	44	26	18
	Urban	14	8	6
45. Mankidi				
	Total	23	12	11
	Rural	11	0	11
	Urban	12	12	0
46. Mankirdia				
	Total	121	84	37
	Rural	121	84	37
47. Matya				
	Total	2,161	1,175	986
	Rural	2,131	1,160	971
	Urban	30	15	15

48. Mirdhas				
	Total	271	135	136
	Rural	264	129	135
	Urban	7	6	1
49. Munda, Munda Lohara, Munda Mahalis				
	Total	32,901	16,935	15,966
	Rural	27,940	14,152	13,788
	Urban	4,961	2,783	2,178
50. Mundari				
	Total	1,140	548	592
	Rural	975	461	514
	Urban	165	87	78
51. Oraon				
	Total	485	267	218
	Rural	192	116	76
	Urban	293	151	142
52. Parenga				
	Total	148	68	80
	Rural	134	66	68
	Urban	14	2	12
53. Pentia				
	Total	162	53	109
	Rural	147	50	97
	Urban	15	3	12
54. Rajuar				
	Total	16	9	7
	Rural	16	9	7
55. Santal				
	Total	4,648	2,592	2,056
	Rural	3,918	2,197	1,721
	Urban	730	395	335

56. Saora, Savar, Saura, Sahara				
	Total	40,253	20,204	20,049
	Rural	37,108	18,515	18,593d
	Urban	3,145	1,689	1,456
57. Shabar, Lodha				
	Total	59,642	30,352	29,290
	Rural	57,738	29,390	28,348
	Urban	1,904	962	942
58. Sounti				
	Total	127	80	47
	Rural	120	73	47
	Urban	7	7	0
59. Tharua				
	Total	10	3	7
	Rural	9	2	7
	Urban	1	1	0
60. Unclassified				
	Total	194	107	87
	Rural	130	73	57
	Urban	64	34	30

Note: 1. All Scheduled Tribes includes figures for 'unclassified'.
2. Tribes having nil return are not shown.

DHENKANAL
(Undivided)

District	*Total/ Rural/ Urban*	*Population*		
		Total	*Males*	*Females*
1	*2*	*3*	*4*	*5*
All Scheduled Tribes				
	Total	2,32,519	1,18,163	1,14,356
	Rural	2,21,162	1,12,092	1,09,070
	Urban	11,357	6,071	5,286
1. Bagata				
	Total	35	16	19
	Rural	16	12	4
	Urban	19	4	15
2. Baiga				
	Total	7	0	7
	Rural	7	0	7
3. Banjara, Banjari				
	Total	20	2	18
	Rural	20	2	18
4. Bathudi				
	Total	45	24	21
	Rural	16	6	10
	Urban	29	18	11
5. Bhottada, Dhotada				
	Total	40	18	22
	Rural	38	16	22
	Urban	2	2	0

6. Bhuiya, Bhuyan				
	Total	7,591	3,220	4,371
	Rural	7,468	3,156	4,312
	Urban	123	64	59
7. Bhumia				
	Total	5	1	4
	Rural	5	1	4
8. Bhumij				
	Total	6,555	3,011	3,544
	Rural	6,533	2,991	3,542
	Urban	22	20	2
9. Bhunjia				
	Total	11	2	9
	Rural	2	1	1
	Urban	9	1	8
10. Binjhal				
	Total	35	21	14
	Rural	27	13	14
	Urban	8	8	0
11. Binjhia, Binjhoa				
	Total	9	9	0
	Urban	9	9	0
12. Birhor				
	Total	5	0	5
	Rural	5	0	5
13. Desua Bhumij				
	Total	2	1	1
	Rural	1	0	1
	Urban	1	1	0
14. Dharua				
	Total	16	5	11
	Rural	11	0	11
	Urban	5	5	0

15. Didayi				
	Total	5	5	0
	Rural	5	5	0
16. Gadaba				
	Total	43	9	34
	Rural	12	2	10
	Urban	31	7	24
17. Gandia				
	Total	61	30	31
	Rural	60	29	31
	Urban	1	1	0
18. Ghara				
	Total	120	73	47
	Rural	104	57	47
	Urban	16	16	0
19. Gond, Gondo				
	Total	23,339	11,439	11,900
	Rural	21,276	10,404	10,872
	Urban	2,063	1,035	1,028
20. Ho				
	Total	9,817	4,668	5,149
	Rural	9,676	4,603	5,073
	Urban	141	65	76
21. Holva				
	Total	20	13	7
	Rural	18	11	7
	Urban	2	2	0
22. Jatapu				
	Total	151	88	63
	Rural	125	74	51
	Urban	26	14	12

23. Juang				
	Total	14,920	7,424	7,496
	Rural	14,345	7,088	7,257
	Urban	575	336	239
24. Kandha Gauda				
	Total	341	225	116
	Rural	323	213	110
	Urban	18	12	6
25. Kawar				
	Total	207	105	102
	Rural	207	105	102
26. Kharia, Kharian				
	Total	2,140	1,102	1,038
	Rural	2,055	1,056	999
	Urban	85	46	39
27. Kharwar				
	Total	39	17	22
	Rural	38	16	22
	Urban	1	1	0
28. Khond, Kond, Kandha, Nanguli Kandha, Sitha Kandha				
	Total	35,407	19,313	16,094
	Rural	32,781	17,895	14,886
	Urban	2,626	1,418	1,208
29. Kisan				
	Total	11,753	6,076	5,677
	Rural	11,697	6,038	5,659
	Urban	56	38	18
30. Kol				
	Total	76	11	65
	Rural	62	4	58
	Urban	14	7	7

31. Kolah Loharas, Kol Loharas

Total	389	229	160
Rural	309	199	110
Urban	80	30	50

32. Kolha

Total	11,585	5,623	5,962
Rural	11,161	5,451	5,710
Urban	424	172	252

33. Koli, Malhar

Total	828	457	371
Rural	827	456	371
Urban	1	1	0

34. Kondadora

Total	116	65	51
Rural	99	58	41
Urban	17	7	10

35. Kora

Total	3,358	1,698	1,660
Rural	3,300	1,678	1,622
Urban	58	20	38

36. Korua

Total	118	54	64
Rural	88	41	47
Urban	30	13	17

37. Kotia

Total	88	62	26
Rural	82	56	26
Urban	6	6	0

38. Lodha

Total	53	27	26
Rural	41	15	26
Urban	12	12	0

39. Madia				
	Total	135	46	89
	Rural	128	39	89
	Urban	7	7	0
40. Mahali				
	Total	641	264	377
	Rural	618	249	369
	Urban	23	15	8
41. Mankirdia				
	Total	103	51	52
	Rural	103	51	52
42. Matya				
	Total	3,186	1,719	1,467
	Rural	3,161	1,704	1,457
	Urban	25	15	10
43. Mirdhas				
	Total	859	375	484
	Rural	840	364	476
	Urban	19	11	8
44. Munda, Munda Lohara, Munda Mahalis				
	Total	26,759	13,987	12,772
	Rural	25,675	13,362	12,313
	Urban	1,084	625	459
45. Mundari				
	Total	450	146	304
	Rural	409	138	271
	Urban	41	8	33
46. Omanatya				
	Total	114	64	50
	Rural	112	62	50
	Urban	2	2	0

47. Oraon

	Total	632	333	299
	Rural	295	175	120
	Urban	337	158	179

48. Parenga

	Total	27	11	16
	Rural	27	11	16

49. Paroja

	Total	81	37	44
	Rural	78	34	44
	Urban	3	3	0

50. Pentia

	Total	218	125	93
	Rural	182	106	76
	Urban	36	19	17

51. Rajuar

	Total	70	45	25
	Rural	61	44	17
	Urban	9	1	8

52. Santal

	Total	8,593	4,610	3,983
	Rural	6,700	3,577	3,123
	Urban	1,893	1,033	860

53. Saora, Savar, Saura, Sahara

	Total	30,711	15,640	15,071
	Rural	30,384	15,401	14,983
	Urban	327	239	88

54. Shabar, Lodha

	Total	30,339	15,451	14,888
	Rural	29,307	14,908	14,399
	Urban	1,032	543	489

55. Sounti				
	Total	181	80	101
	Rural	181	80	101
56. Tharua				
	Total	66	34	32
	Rural	58	34	24
	Urban	8	0	8
57. Unclassified				
	Total	4	2	2
	Rural	3	1	2
	Urban	1	1	0

Note: 1. All Scheduled Tribes includes figures for 'unclassified'.
2. Tribes having nil return are not shown.

GANJAM
(Undivided)

District	*Total/ Rural/ Urban*	*Population*		
		Total	*Males*	*Females*
1	*2*	*3*	*4*	*5*
All Scheduled Tribes				
	Total	2,96,845	1,45,761	1,51,084
	Rural	2,93,560	1,43,817	1,49,743
	Urban	3,285	1,944	1,341
1. Bagata				
	Total	74	41	33
	Rural	51	32	19
	Urban	23	9	14
2. Baiga				
	Total	1	0	1
	Rural	1	0	1
3. Banjara, Banjari				
	Total	9	8	1
	Rural	1	0	1
	Urban	8	8	0
4. Bathudi				
	Total	174	57	117
	Rural	164	52	112
	Urban	10	5	5
5. Bhottada, Dhotada				
	Total	12	4	8
	Rural	8	0	8
	Urban	4	4	0

6. Bhuiya, Bhuyan				
	Total	629	300	329
	Rural	582	270	312
	Urban	47	30	17
7. Bhumia				
	Total	1	0	1
	Rural	1	0	1
8. Bhumij				
	Total	16	12	4
	Rural	15	11	4
	Urban	1	1	0
9. Bhunjia				
	Total	22	9	13
	Rural	22	9	13
10. Binjhal				
	Total	176	116	60
	Rural	174	114	60
	Urban	2	2	0
11. Binjhia, Binjhoa				
	Total	14	5	9
	Rural	6	4	2
	Urban	8	1	7
12. Bondo Poraja				
	Total	31	19	12
	Rural	22	10	12
	Urban	9	9	0
13. Chenchu				
	Total	10	10	0
	Rural	10	10	0
14. Dal				
	Total	51	30	21
	Rural	51	30	21

15. Desua Bhumij				
	Total	86	32	54
	Rural	86	32	54
16. Dharua				
	Total	27	26	1
	Rural	18	17	1
	Urban	9	9	0
17. Didayi				
	Total	3	3	0
	Rural	2	2	0
	Urban	1	1	0
18. Gadaba				
	Total	15	5	10
	Rural	10	0	10
	Urban	5	5	0
19. Ghara				
	Total	10	0	10
	Rural	10	0	10
20. Gond, Gondo				
	Total	165	103	62
	Rural	160	98	62
	Urban	5	5	0
21. Ho				
	Total	16	6	10
	Rural	14	4	10
	Urban	2	2	0
22. Jatapu				
	Total	2,675	1,461	1,214
	Rural	2,674	1,460	1,214
	Urban	1	1	0
23. Juang				
	Total	5	4	1
	Urban	5	4	1

24. Kandha Gauda				
	Total	4,019	2,076	1,943
	Rural	3,757	1,918	1,839
	Urban	262	158	104
25. Kawar				
	Total	24	9	15
	Rural	20	5	15
	Urban	4	4	0
26. Kharia, Kharian				
	Total	38	11	27
	Rural	25	10	15
	Urban	13	1	12
27. Kharwar				
	Total	145	78	67
	Rural	145	78	67
28. Khond, Kond, Kandha, Nanguli Kandha, Sitha Kandha				
	Total	71,589	34,667	36,922
	Rural	70,900	34,253	36,647
	Urban	689	414	275
29. Kisan				
	Total	57	16	41
	Rural	43	2	41
	Urban	14	14	0
30. Kol				
	Total	51	23	28
	Rural	50	22	28
	Urban	1	1	0
31. Kolah Loharas, Kol Loharas				
	Total	32	20	12
	Rural	32	20	12

32. Kolha				
	Total	251	117	134
	Rural	135	64	71
	Urban	116	53	63
33. Koli, Malhar				
	Total	471	176	295
	Rural	55	13	42
	Urban	416	163	253
34. Kondadora				
	Total	404	224	180
	Rural	392	223	169
	Urban	12	1	11
35. Kora				
	Total	9	9	0
	Urban	9	9	0
36. Korua				
	Total	44	22	22
	Rural	35	21	14
	Urban	9	1	8
37. Kotia				
	Total	12	8	4
	Rural	12	8	4
38. Koya				
	Total	78	15	63
	Rural	30	9	21
	Urban	48	6	42
39. Kulis				
	Total	121	68	53
	Rural	115	63	52
	Urban	6	5	1
40. Lodha				
	Total	181	91	90
	Rural	181	91	90

41. Madia				
	Total	40	22	18
	Rural	9	1	8
	Urban	31	21	10
42. Mahali				
	Total	104	74	30
	Rural	81	51	30
	Urban	23	23	0
43. Mankidi				
	Total	29	27	2
	Rural	24	22	2
	Urban	5	5	0
44. Mankirdia				
	Total	10	0	10
	Rural	10	0	10
45. Matya				
	Total	1,119	535	584
	Rural	972	461	511
	Urban	147	74	73
46. Munda, Munda Lohara, Munda Mahalis				
	Total	524	300	224
	Rural	463	263	200
	Urban	61	37	24
47. Mundari				
	Total	77	52	25
	Rural	67	42	25
	Urban	10	10	0
48. Omanatya				
	Total	4	2	2
	Rural	4	2	2
49. Oraon				
	Total	207	100	107
	Rural	192	85	107
	Urban	15	15	0

50. Parenga				
	Total	28	5	23
	Rural	28	5	23
51. Paroja				
	Total	79	49	30
	Rural	68	38	30
	Urban	11	11	0
52. Pentia				
	Total	17	3	14
	Rural	15	1	14
	Urban	2	2	0
53. Rajuar				
	Total	56	38	18
	Rural	55	37	18
	Urban	1	1	0
54. Santal				
	Total	259	152	107
	Rural	165	108	57
	Urban	94	44	50
55. Saora, Savar, Saura, Sahara				
	Total	77,694	38,153	39,541
	Rural	77,343	37,966	39,377
	Urban	351	187	164
56. Shabar, Lodha				
	Total	1,33,471	65,688	67,783
	Rural	1,32,714	65,122	67,592
	Urban	757	566	191
57. Sounti				
	Total	794	395	399
	Rural	774	381	393
	Urban	20	14	6

58. Tharua				
	Total	12	0	12
	Rural	12	0	12
59. Unclassified				
	Total	573	285	288
	Rural	555	277	278
	Urban	18	8	10

Note: 1. All Scheduled Tribes includes figures for 'unclassified'.
2. Tribes having nil return are not shown.

KALAHANDI
(Undivided)

District	*Total/ Rural/ Urban*	*Population*		
		Total	*Males*	*Females*
1	*2*	*3*	*4*	*5*
All Scheduled Tribes				
	Total	4,95,425	2,44,461	2,50,964
	Rural	4,88,490	2,40,949	2,47,541
	Urban	6,935	3,512	3,423
1. Bagata				
	Total	68	31	37
	Rural	68	31	37
2. Baiga				
	Total	64	52	12
	Rural	64	52	12
3. Banjara, Banjari				
	Total	6,168	3,153	3,015
	Rural	6,112	3,126	2,986
	Urban	56	27	29
4. Bathudi				
	Total	115	23	92
	Rural	115	23	92
5. Bhottada, Dhotada				
	Total	33,316	14,443	18,873
	Rural	33,309	14,436	18,873
	Urban	7	7	0

6. Bhuiya, Bhuyan				
	Total	1,013	495	518
	Rural	983	481	502
	Urban	30	14	16
7. Bhumia				
	Total	100	61	39
	Rural	100	61	39
8. Bhumij				
	Total	98	55	43
	Rural	96	53	43
	Urban	2	2	0
9. Bhunjia				
	Total	7,142	3,579	3,563
	Rural	7,101	3,557	3,544
	Urban	41	22	19
10. Binjhal				
	Total	5,869	2,926	2,943
	Rural	5,818	2,895	2,923
	Urban	51	31	20
11. Binjhia, Binjhoa				
	Total	179	98	81
	Rural	179	98	81
12. Birhor				
	Total	165	109	56
	Rural	161	105	56
	Urban	4	4	0
13. Bondo Poraja				
	Total	47	11	36
	Rural	45	11	34
	Urban	2	0	2

14. Chenchu				
	Total	27	19	8
	Rural	27	19	8
15. Dal				
	Total	3,406	1,881	1,525
	Rural	3,406	1,881	1,525
16. Desua Bhumij				
	Total	72	58	14
	Rural	72	58	14
17. Dharua				
	Total	97	46	51
	Rural	96	45	51
	Urban	1	1	0
18. Gadaba				
	Total	40	30	10
	Rural	40	30	10
19. Gandia				
	Total	81	42	39
	Rural	68	40	28
	Urban	13	2	11
20. Ghara				
	Total	168	70	98
	Rural	168	70	98
21. Gond, Gondo				
	Total	1,72,686	84,860	87,826
	Rural	1,71,698	84,376	87,322
	Urban	988	484	504
22. Ho				
	Total	40	11	29
	Rural	39	10	29
	Urban	1	1	0

23. Holva				
	Total	720	379	341
	Rural	720	379	341
24. Jatapu				
	Total	43	32	11
	Rural	34	23	11
	Urban	9	9	0
25. Juang				
	Total	34	18	16
	Rural	34	18	16
26. Kandha Gauda				
	Total	742	362	380
	Rural	287	164	123
	Urban	455	198	257
27. Kawar				
	Total	1,390	707	683
	Rural	1,377	704	673
	Urban	13	3	10
28. Kharia, Kharian				
	Total	1,006	522	484
	Rural	980	507	473
	Urban	26	15	11
29. Kharwar				
	Total	57	25	32
	Rural	47	24	23
	Urban	10	1	9
30. Khond, Kond, Kandha, Nanguli Kandha, Sitha Kandha				
	Total	1,46,225	73,957	72,268
	Rural	1,43,300	72,535	70,765
	Urban	2,925	1,422	1,503

31. Kisan

	Total	188	83	105
	Rural	183	81	102
	Urban	5	2	3

32. Kol

	Total	190	93	97
	Rural	187	90	97
	Urban	3	3	0

33. Kolah Loharas, Kol Loharas

	Total	1,868	938	930
	Rural	1,799	920	879
	Urban	69	18	51

34. Kolha

	Total	794	348	446
	Rural	794	348	446

35. Koli, Malhar

	Total	49	23	26
	Rural	37	11	26
	Urban	12	12	0

36. Kondadora

	Total	1,032	656	376
	Rural	1,029	653	376
	Urban	3	3	0

37. Kora

	Total	109	60	49
	Rural	109	60	49

38. Korua

	Total	12	11	1
	Rural	12	11	1

39. Kotia

	Total	8,089	4,048	4,041
	Rural	8,089	4,048	4,041

40. Koya				
	Total	7	7	0
	Rural	7	7	0
41. Kulis				
	Total	19	11	8
	Rural	10	2	8
	Urban	9	9	0
42. Lodha				
	Total	1	0	1
	Rural	1	0	1
43. Madia				
	Total	1	0	1
	Rural	1	0	1
44. Mahali				
	Total	449	252	197
	Rural	447	251	196
	Urban	2	1	1
45. Mankidi				
	Total	115	70	45
	Rural	115	70	45
46. Mankirdia				
	Total	388	212	176
	Rural	384	210	174
	Urban	4	2	2
47. Matya				
	Total	6	1	5
	Rural	1	0	1
	Urban	5	1	4
48. Mirdhas				
	Total	1,265	688	577
	Rural	1,222	659	563
	Urban	43	29	14

49. Munda, Munda Lohara, Munda Mahalis

Total	5,940	2,743	3,197
Rural	5,709	2,655	3,054
Urban	231	88	143

50. Mundari

Total	111	83	28
Rural	111	83	28

51. Omanatya

Total	50	32	18
Rural	50	32	18

52. Oraon

Total	124	72	52
Rural	98	58	40
Urban	26	14	12

53. Parenga

Total	39	15	24
Rural	39	15	24

54. Paroja

Total	28,217	13,897	14,320
Rural	28,212	13,892	14,320
Urban	5	5	0

55. Pentia

Total	18	15	3
Rural	18	15	3

56. Santal

Total	221	138	83
Rural	193	113	80
Urban	28	25	3

57. Saora, Savar, Saura, Sahara

Total	4,097	1,880	2,217
Rural	3,967	1,786	2,181
Urban	130	94	36

58. Shabar, Lodha				
	Total	60,236	29,702	30,534
	Rural	58,542	28,763	29,779
	Urban	1,694	939	755
59. Sounti				
	Total	136	59	77
	Rural	110	41	69
	Urban	26	18	8
60. Tharua				
	Total	412	239	173
	Rural	406	233	173
	Urban	6	6	0
61. Unclassified				
	Total	64	30	34
	Rural	64	30	34

Note: 1. All Scheduled Tribes includes figures for 'unclassified'.
2. Tribes having nil return are not shown.

KENDUJHAR
(Undivided)

District	*Total/ Rural/ Urban*	*Population*		
		Total	*Males*	*Females*
1	*2*	*3*	*4*	*5*
All Scheduled Tribes				
	Total	5,95,184	2,97,951	2,97,233
	Rural	5,54,633	2,76,856	2,77,777
	Urban	40,551	21,095	19,456
1. Bagata				
	Total	386	209	177
	Rural	348	181	167
	Urban	38	28	10
2. Baiga				
	Total	126	56	70
	Rural	115	54	61
	Urban	11	2	9
3. Banjara, Banjari				
	Total	109	62	47
	Rural	89	51	38
	Urban	20	11	9
4. Bathudi				
	Total	59,548	29,811	29,737
	Rural	58,387	29,162	29,225
	Urban	1,161	649	512
5. Bhottada, Dhotada				
	Total	163	75	88
	Rural	148	61	87
	Urban	15	14	1

6. Bhuiya, Bhuyan				
	Total	73,366	35,886	37,480
	Rural	68,541	33,331	35,210
	Urban	4,825	2,555	2,270
7. Bhumia				
	Total	145	90	55
	Rural	115	70	45
	Urban	30	20	10
8. Bhumij				
	Total	5,040	2,642	2,398
	Rural	4,173	2,191	1,982
	Urban	867	451	416
9. Bhunjia				
	Total	258	130	128
	Rural	142	37	105
	Urban	116	93	23
10. Binjhal				
	Total	2	2	0
	Rural	1	1	0
	Urban	1	1	0
11. Binjhia, Binjhoa				
	Total	24	15	9
	Rural	18	9	9
	Urban	6	6	0
12. Birhor				
	Total	249	129	120
	Rural	125	60	65
	Urban	124	69	55
13. Bondo Poraja				
	Total	12	11	1
	Rural	12	11	1

14. Chenchu				
	Total	26	23	3
	Rural	11	10	1
	Urban	15	13	2
15. Dal				
	Total	342	122	220
	Rural	232	77	155
	Urban	110	45	65
16. Desua Bhumij				
	Total	105	81	24
	Rural	104	81	23
	Urban	1	0	1
17. Didayi				
	Total	11	1	10
	Rural	10	0	10
	Urban	1	1	0
18. Gandia				
	Total	170	82	88
	Rural	170	82	88
19. Ghara				
	Total	33	16	17
	Rural	32	15	17
	Urban	1	1	0
20. Gond, Gondo				
	Total	65,623	33,280	32,343
	Rural	60,805	30,994	29,811
	Urban	4,818	2,286	2,532
21. Ho				
	Total	8,067	4,074	3,993
	Rural	7,713	3,886	3,827
	Urban	354	188	166

22. Holva				
	Total	311	139	172
	Rural	310	138	172
	Urban	1	1	0
23. Jatapu				
	Total	293	171	122
	Rural	282	169	113
	Urban	11	2	9
24. Juang				
	Total	19,109	9,010	10,099
	Rural	19,075	8,994	10,081
	Urban	34	16	18
25. Kandha Gauda				
	Total	218	106	112
	Rural	205	103	102
	Urban	13	3	10
26. Kawar				
	Total	194	126	68
	Rural	194	126	68
27. Kharia, Kharian				
	Total	631	345	286
	Rural	582	320	262
	Urban	49	25	24
28. Kharwar				
	Total	12	1	11
	Rural	11	0	11
	Urban	1	1	0
29. Khond, Kond, Kandha, Nanguli Kandha, Sitha Kandha				
	Total	2,620	1,425	1,195
	Rural	2,406	1,309	1,097
	Urban	214	116	98

30. Kisan				
	Total	4,153	2,042	2,111
	Rural	4,123	2,029	2,094
	Urban	30	13	17
31. Kol				
	Total	960	502	458
	Rural	912	470	442
	Urban	48	32	16
32. Kolah Loharas, Kol Loharas				
	Total	994	471	523
	Rural	586	273	313
	Urban	408	198	210
33. Kolha				
	Total	1,48,777	75,419	73,358
	Rural	1,37,359	69,431	67,928
	Urban	11,418	5,988	5,430
34. Koli, Malhar				
	Total	384	141	243
	Rural	371	138	233
	Urban	13	3	10
35. Kondadora				
	Total	628	374	254
	Rural	554	348	206
	Urban	74	26	48
36. Kora				
	Total	1,554	857	697
	Rural	1,525	837	688
	Urban	29	20	9
37. Korua				
	Total	90	68	22
	Rural	32	20	12
	Urban	58	48	10

38. Kotia				
	Total	77	31	46
	Rural	52	15	37
	Urban	25	16	9
39. Koya				
	Total	113	54	59
	Rural	94	44	50
	Urban	19	10	9
40. Kulis				
	Total	28	11	17
	Rural	17	7	10
	Urban	11	4	7
41. Lodha				
	Total	428	184	244
	Rural	335	136	199
	Urban	93	48	45
42. Mahali				
	Total	321	110	211
	Rural	290	104	186
	Urban	31	6	25
43. Mankidi				
	Total	205	114	91
	Rural	155	91	64
	Urban	50	23	27
44. Mankirdia				
	Total	111	75	36
	Rural	92	60	32
	Urban	19	15	4
45. Matya				
	Total	1,882	852	1,030
	Rural	1,839	837	1,002
	Urban	43	15	28

46. Mirdhas

	Total	73	44	29
	Rural	54	34	20
	Urban	19	10	9

47. Munda, Munda Lohara, Munda Mahalis

	Total	42,366	21,320	21,046
	Rural	34,220	17,020	17,200
	Urban	8,146	4,300	3,846

48. Mundari

	Total	2,406	1,108	1,298
	Rural	1,879	877	1,002
	Urban	527	231	296

49. Omanatya

	Total	29	2	27
	Rural	21	2	19
	Urban	8	0	8

50. Oraon

	Total	4,651	2,269	2,382
	Rural	3,739	1,831	1,908
	Urban	912	438	474

51. Parenga

	Total	80	22	58
	Rural	70	19	51
	Urban	10	3	7

52. Paroja

	Total	327	156	171
	Rural	289	140	149
	Urban	38	16	22

53. Pentia

	Total	696	340	356
	Rural	628	308	320
	Urban	68	32	36

54. Rajuar				
	Total	180	47	133
	Rural	139	24	115
	Urban	41	23	18
55. Santal				
	Total	46,368	24,130	22,238
	Rural	43,772	22,690	21,082
	Urban	2,596	1,440	1,156
56. Saora, Savar, Saura, Sahara				
	Total	10,549	5,461	5,088
	Rural	10,237	5,310	4,927
	Urban	312	151	161
57. Shabar, Lodha				
	Total	18,768	9,387	9,381
	Rural	17,442	8,713	8,729
	Urban	1,326	674	652
58. Sounti				
	Total	70,641	34,180	36,461
	Rural	69,314	33,471	35,843
	Urban	1,327	709	618
59. Tharua				
	Total	144	56	88
	Rural	129	50	79
	Urban	15	6	9
60. Unclassified				
	Total	8	4	4
	Rural	8	4	4

Note: 1. All Scheduled Tribes includes figures for 'unclassified'.
2. Tribes having nil return are not shown.

KORAPUT
(Undivided)

District	*Total/ Rural/ Urban*	*Population*		
		Total	*Males*	*Females*
1	*2*	*3*	*4*	*5*
All Scheduled Tribes				
	Total	16,36,079	8,11,892	8,24,187
	Rural	15,87,275	7,87,709	7,99,566
	Urban	48,804	24,183	24,621
1. Bagata				
	Total	498	269	229
	Rural	477	262	215
	Urban	21	7	14
2. Baiga				
	Total	147	81	66
	Rural	124	76	48
	Urban	23	5	18
3. Banjara, Banjari				
	Total	2,645	1,241	1,404
	Rural	2,632	1,231	1,401
	Urban	13	10	3
4. Bathudi				
	Total	881	514	367
	Rural	842	490	352
	Urban	39	24	15
5. Bhottada, Dhotada				
	Total	2,69,993	1,21,564	1,48,429
	Rural	2,64,912	1,18,716	1,46,196
	Urban	5,081	2,848	2,233

6. Bhuiya, Bhuyan				
	Total	5,785	2,085	3,700
	Rural	5,617	2,019	3,598
	Urban	168	66	102
7. Bhumia				
	Total	1,08,784	56,267	52,517
	Rural	1,08,338	56,055	52,283
	Urban	446	212	234
8. Bhumij				
	Total	1,083	434	649
	Rural	966	354	612
	Urban	117	80	37
9. Bhunjia				
	Total	2,254	1,174	1,080
	Rural	2,167	1,161	1,006
	Urban	87	13	74
10. Binjhal				
	Total	255	139	116
	Rural	251	135	116
	Urban	4	4	0
11. Binjhia, Binjhoa				
	Total	307	159	148
	Rural	303	155	148
	Urban	4	4	0
12. Bondo Poraja				
	Total	6,863	3,257	3,606
	Rural	6,850	3,247	3,603
	Urban	13	10	3
13. Chenchu				
	Total	152	73	79
	Rural	152	73	79

14. Dal				
	Total	489	228	261
	Rural	486	225	261
	Urban	3	3	0
15. Desua Bhumij				
	Total	137	45	92
	Rural	132	40	92
	Urban	5	5	0
16. Dharua				
	Total	10,209	5,607	4,602
	Rural	10,194	5,594	4,600
	Urban	15	13	2
17. Didayi				
	Total	5,324	2,627	2,697
	Rural	5,321	2,625	2,696
	Urban	3	2	1
18. Gadaba				
	Total	66,781	33,866	32,915
	Rural	63,538	32,066	31,472
	Urban	3,243	1,800	1,443
19. Gandia				
	Total	2,489	1,227	1,262
	Rural	2,467	1,206	1,261
	Urban	22	21	1
20. Ghara				
	Total	329	134	195
	Rural	328	133	195
	Urban	1	1	0
21. Gond, Gondo				
	Total	1,26,526	64,597	61,929
	Rural	1,26,416	64,489	61,927
	Urban	110	108	2

22. Ho				
	Total	148	64	84
	Rural	123	52	71
	Urban	25	12	13
23. Holva				
	Total	11,732	5,509	6,223
	Rural	10,185	5,476	4,709
	Urban	1,547	33	1,514
24. Jatapu				
	Total	4,186	2,008	2,178
	Rural	4,002	1,895	2,107
	Urban	184	113	71
25. Juang				
	Total	136	82	54
	Rural	134	80	54
	Urban	2	2	0
26. Kandha Gauda				
	Total	3,966	2,169	1,797
	Rural	3,912	2,131	1,781
	Urban	54	38	16
27. Kawar				
	Total	228	108	120
	Rural	221	101	120
	Urban	7	7	0
28. Kharia, Kharian				
	Total	310	153	157
	Rural	158	70	88
	Urban	152	83	69
29. Khond, Kond, Kandha, Nanguli Kandha, Sitha Kandha				
	Total	4,14,206	2,14,505	1,99,701
	Rural	4,00,341	2,05,199	1,95,142
	Urban	13,865	9,306	4,559

30. Kisan

Total	392	210	182
Rural	314	161	153
Urban	78	49	29

31. Kol

Total	67	64	3
Rural	64	61	3
Urban	3	3	0

32. Kolah Loharas, Kol Loharas

Total	1,227	583	644
Rural	1,220	576	644
Urban	7	7	0

33. Kolha

Total	1,632	865	767
Rural	1,585	844	741
Urban	47	21	26

34. Koli, Malhar

Total	108	31	77
Rural	103	26	77
Urban	5	5	0

35. Kondadora

Total	16,000	8,720	7,280
Rural	15,160	8,103	7,057
Urban	840	617	223

36. Kora

Total	1,244	767	477
Rural	1,240	763	477
Urban	4	4	0

37. Korua

Total	93	32	61
Rural	55	25	30
Urban	38	7	31

38. Kotia				
	Total	14,978	7,690	7,288
	Rural	14,820	7,627	7,193
	Urban	158	63	95
39. Koya				
	Total	1,41,509	73,774	67,735
	Rural	1,41,160	73,654	67,506
	Urban	349	120	229
40. Kulis				
	Total	403	193	210
	Rural	399	189	210
	Urban	4	4	0
41. Lodha				
	Total	1,209	352	857
	Rural	1,207	350	857
	Urban	2	2	0
42. Madia				
	Total	486	269	217
	Rural	481	264	217
	Urban	5	5	0
43. Mahali				
	Total	428	223	205
	Rural	390	212	178
	Urban	38	11	27
44. Mankidi				
	Total	191	78	113
	Rural	189	76	113
	Urban	2	2	0
45. Mankirdia				
	Total	65	29	36
	Rural	65	29	36

46. Matya

Total	2,781	1,167	1,614
Rural	2,755	1,159	1,596
Urban	26	8	18

47. Mirdhas

Total	139	71	68
Rural	123	62	61
Urban	16	9	7

48. Munda, Munda Lohara, Munda Mahalis

Total	2,296	526	1,770
Rural	2,287	518	1,769
Urban	9	8	1

49. Mundari

Total	365	144	221
Rural	324	135	189
Urban	41	9	32

50. Omanatya

Total	24,489	12,653	11,836
Rural	24,367	12,627	11,740
Urban	122	26	96

51. Oraon

Total	604	295	309
Rural	401	219	182
Urban	203	76	127

52. Parenga

Total	4,673	2,488	2,185
Rural	4,641	2,474	2,167
Urban	32	14	18

53. Paroja

Total	3,22,545	1,57,991	1,64,554
Rural	3,04,027	1,50,947	1,53,080
Urban	18,518	7,044	11,474

54. Pentia	Total	8,764	4,791	3,973
	Rural	8,749	4,781	3,968
	Urban	15	10	5
55. Rajuar	Total	256	196	60
	Rural	254	195	59
	Urban	2	1	1
56. Santal	Total	7,932	3,440	4,492
	Rural	7,416	3,200	4,216
	Urban	516	240	276
57. Saora, Savar, Saura, Sahara	Total	21,064	8,044	13,020
	Rural	19,843	7,647	12,196
	Urban	1,221	397	824
58. Shabar, Lodha	Total	12,813	5,737	7,076
	Rural	11,590	5,155	6,435
	Urban	1,223	582	641
59. Sounti	Total	108	60	48
	Rural	103	56	47
	Urban	5	4	1
60. Tharua	Total	59	58	1
	Rural	59	58	1
61. Unclassified	Total	316	165	151
	Rural	295	160	135
	Urban	21	5	16

Note: 1. All Scheduled Tribes includes figures for 'unclassified'.
2. Tribes having nil return are not shown.

MAYURBHANJ
(Undivided)

District	*Total/ Rural/ Urban*	*Population*		
		Total	*Males*	*Females*
1	*2*	*3*	*4*	*5*
All Scheduled Tribes				
	Total	10,90,626	5,46,349	5,44,277
	Rural	10,69,312	5,35,216	5,34,096
	Urban	21,314	11,133	10,181
1. Bagata				
	Total	460	218	242
	Rural	450	215	235
	Urban	10	3	7
2. Baiga				
	Total	681	339	342
	Rural	681	339	342
3. Banjara, Banjari				
	Total	156	98	58
	Rural	155	97	58
	Urban	1	1	0
4. Bathudi				
	Total	95,818	47,522	48,296
	Rural	92,273	45,632	46,641
	Urban	3,545	1,890	1,655
5. Bhottada, Dhotada				
	Total	103	73	30
	Rural	102	72	30
	Urban	1	1	0

6. Bhuiya, Bhuyan	Total	47,472	23,905	23,567
	Rural	46,794	23,502	23,292
	Urban	678	403	275
7. Bhumia	Total	156	86	70
	Rural	156	86	70
8. Bhumij	Total	1,06,659	53,600	53,059
	Rural	1,02,911	51,653	51,258
	Urban	3,748	1,947	1,801
9. Bhunjia	Total	932	484	448
	Rural	911	472	439
	Urban	21	12	9
10. Binjhal	Total	231	104	127
	Rural	231	104	127
11. Binjhia, Binjhoa	Total	9	4	5
	Rural	9	4	5
12. Birhor	Total	1	0	1
	Rural	1	0	1
13. Bondo Poraja	Total	45	33	12
	Rural	45	33	12
14. Chenchu	Total	3	1	2
	Rural	3	1	2

15. Dal				
	Total	316	168	148
	Rural	316	168	148
16. Desua Bhumij				
	Total	250	131	119
	Rural	242	131	111
	Urban	8	0	8
17. Dharua				
	Total	371	187	184
	Rural	371	187	184
18. Didayi				
	Total	61	13	48
	Rural	61	13	48
19. Gandia				
	Total	403	176	227
	Rural	400	174	226
	Urban	3	2	1
20. Ghara				
	Total	18	4	14
	Rural	18	4	14
21. Gond, Gondo				
	Total	22,196	10,984	11,212
	Rural	22,130	10,943	11,187
	Urban	66	41	25
22. Ho				
	Total	25,843	11,787	14,056
	Rural	25,506	11,578	13,928
	Urban	337	209	128
23. Holva				
	Total	337	194	143
	Rural	336	193	143
	Urban	1	1	0

24. Jatapu				
	Total	810	385	425
	Rural	775	358	417
	Urban	35	27	8
25. Juang				
	Total	255	124	131
	Rural	252	122	130
	Urban	3	2	1
26. Kandha Gauda				
	Total	1,230	655	575
	Rural	1,225	650	575
	Urban	5	5	0
27. Kawar				
	Total	373	193	180
	Rural	357	185	172
	Urban	16	8	8
28. Kharia, Kharian				
	Total	15,666	7,767	7,899
	Rural	15,405	7,656	7,749
	Urban	261	111	150
29. Khond, Kond, Kandha, Nanguli Kandha, Sitha Kandha				
	Total	967	541	426
	Rural	927	502	425
	Urban	40	39	1
30. Kisan				
	Total	520	335	185
	Rural	511	334	177
	Urban	9	1	8
31. Kol				
	Total	216	130	86
	Rural	210	124	86
	Urban	6	6	0

32. Kolah Loharas, Kol Loharas

Total	2,139	1,142	997
Rural	2,088	1,113	975
Urban	51	29	22

33. Kolha

Total	1,82,551	89,662	92,889
Rural	1,81,193	88,889	92,304
Urban	1,358	773	585

34. Koli, Malhar

Total	154	84	70
Rural	151	82	69
Urban	3	2	1

35. Kondadora

Total	351	108	243
Rural	350	107	243
Urban	1	1	0

36. Kora

Total	622	293	329
Rural	622	293	329

37. Korua

Total	191	99	92
Rural	112	81	31
Urban	79	18	61

38. Kotia

Total	342	141	201
Rural	333	141	192
Urban	9	0	9

39. Koya

Total	25	25	0
Rural	25	25	0

40. Kulis

Total	38	1	37
Rural	38	1	37

41. Lodha				
	Total	2,405	1,287	1,118
	Rural	2,405	1,287	1,118
42. Madia				
	Total	57	15	42
	Rural	56	15	41
	Urban	1	0	1
43. Mahali				
	Total	6,778	3,473	3,305
	Rural	6,735	3,455	3,280
	Urban	43	18	25
44. Mankidi				
	Total	392	174	218
	Rural	392	174	218
45. Mankirdia				
	Total	321	156	165
	Rural	321	156	165
46. Matya				
	Total	180	115	65
	Rural	86	53	33
	Urban	94	62	32
47. Mirdhas				
	Total	16	7	9
	Rural	16	7	9
48. Munda, Munda Lohara, Munda Mahalis				
	Total	37,946	19,323	18,623
	Rural	37,591	19,119	18,472
	Urban	355	204	151
49. Mundari				
	Total	5,988	2,784	3,204
	Rural	5,863	2,739	3,124
	Urban	125	45	80

50. Omanatya				
	Total	55	43	12
	Rural	54	42	12
	Urban	1	1	0
51. Oraon				
	Total	3,716	1,820	1,896
	Rural	3,712	1,816	1,896
	Urban	4	4	0
52. Parenga				
	Total	88	26	62
	Rural	80	26	54
	Urban	8	0	8
53. Paroja				
	Total	317	81	236
	Rural	310	80	230
	Urban	7	1	6
54. Pentia				
	Total	586	320	266
	Rural	576	318	258
	Urban	10	2	8
55. Rajuar				
	Total	2,154	1,008	1,146
	Rural	2,138	1,006	1,132
	Urban	16	2	14
56. Santal				
	Total	4,74,051	2,40,402	2,33,649
	Rural	4,66,349	2,36,455	2,29,894
	Urban	7,702	3,947	3,755
57. Saora, Savar, Saura, Sahara				
	Total	4,321	1,944	2,377
	Rural	3,740	1,675	2,065
	Urban	581	269	12

58. Shabar, Lodha

	Total	7,493	3,603	3,890
	Rural	6,488	3,074	3,414
	Urban	1,005	529	476

59. Sounti

	Total	19,772	9,564	10,208
	Rural	19,100	9,216	9,884
	Urban	672	348	324

60. Tharua

	Total	161	64	97
	Rural	157	63	94
	Urban	4	1	3

61. Unclassified

	Total	14,858	8,344	6,514
	Rural	14,467	8,176	6,291
	Urban	391	168	223

Note: 1. All Scheduled Tribes includes figures for 'unclassified'.
2. Tribes having nil return are not shown.

PHULABANI
(Undivided)

District	*Total/ Rural/ Urban*	*Population*		
		Total	*Males*	*Females*
1	*2*	*3*	*4*	*5*
All Scheduled Tribes				
	Total	3,22,408	1,59,310	1,63,098
	Rural	3,17,737	1,56,846	1,60,891
	Urban	4,671	2,464	2,207
1. Bagata				
	Total	16	5	11
	Rural	11	0	11
	Urban	5	5	0
2. Baiga				
	Total	1	0	1
	Rural	1	0	1
3. Banjara, Banjari				
	Total	115	63	52
	Rural	115	63	52
4. Bathudi				
	Total	4	4	0
	Rural	4	4	0
5. Bhottada, Dhotada				
	Total	14	2	12
	Rural	14	2	12
6. Bhuiya, Bhuyan				
	Total	49	30	19
	Rural	32	21	11
	Urban	17	9	8

7. Bhumij				
	Total	64	24	40
	Rural	64	24	40
8. Bhunjia				
	Total	1	1	0
	Urban	1	1	0
9. Binjhal				
	Total	15	11	4
	Rural	14	10	4
	Urban	1	1	0
10. Birhor				
	Total	10	0	10
	Rural	10	0	10
11. Dharua				
	Total	51	41	10
	Rural	51	41	10
12. Gandia				
	Total	1	1	0
	Rural	1	1	0
13. Ghara				
	Total	86	22	64
	Rural	75	22	53
	Urban	11	0	11
14. Gond, Gondo				
	Total	13,619	6,612	7,007
	Rural	13,379	6,494	6,885
	Urban	240	118	122
15. Ho				
	Total	58	46	12
	Rural	53	41	12
	Urban	5	5	0

16. Holva

Total	16	6	10
Rural	11	1	10
Urban	5	5	0

17. Jatapu

Total	11	11	0
Rural	11	11	0

18. Kandha Gauda

Total	3,523	1,715	1,808
Rural	3,420	1,640	1,780
Urban	103	75	28

19. Kawar

Total	1	1	0
Rural	1	1	0

20. Kharia, Kharian

Total	752	342	410
Rural	750	340	410
Urban	2	2	0

21. Kharwar

Total	13	2	11
Rural	13	2	11

22. Khond, Kond, Kandha, Nanguli Kandha, Sitha Kandha

Total	2,90,388	1,43,546	1,46,842
Rural	2,86,203	1,41,352	1,44,851
Urban	4,185	2,194	1,991

23. Kisan

Total	166	43	123
Rural	166	43	123

24. Kol

Total	218	52	166
Rural	218	52	166

25. Kolah Loharas, Kol Loharas				
	Total	264	145	119
	Rural	264	145	119
26. Kolha				
	Total	661	339	322
	Rural	644	339	305
	Urban	17	0	17
27. Koli, Malhar				
	Total	131	39	92
	Rural	119	34	85
	Urban	12	5	7
28. Kondadora				
	Total	110	70	40
	Rural	110	70	40
29. Kora				
	Total	262	119	143
	Rural	262	119	143
30. Korua				
	Total	32	20	12
	Rural	32	20	12
31. Kotia				
	Total	4,653	2,315	2,338
	Rural	4,653	2,315	2,338
32. Kulis				
	Total	96	60	36
	Rural	96	60	36
33. Lodha				
	Total	4	1	3
	Rural	4	1	3
34. Madia				
	Total	1	0	1
	Rural	1	0	1

35. Mahali				
	Total	11	0	11
	Rural	11	0	11
36. Mankirdia				
	Total	12	2	10
	Rural	12	2	10
37. Mirdhas				
	Total	739	381	358
	Rural	739	381	358
38. Munda, Munda Lohara, Munda Mahalis				
	Total	888	508	380
	Rural	886	508	378
	Urban	2	0	2
39. Mundari				
	Total	64	50	14
	Rural	59	45	14
	Urban	5	5	0
40. Omanatya				
	Total	382	192	190
	Rural	381	191	190
	Urban	1	1	0
41. Oraon				
	Total	26	1	25
	Rural	26	1	25
42. Paroja				
	Total	2	0	2
	Rural	2	0	2
43. Pentia				
	Total	22	18	4
	Rural	21	17	4
	Urban	1	1	0

44. Rajuar	Total	2	0	2
	Rural	2	0	2
45. Santal	Total	95	52	43
	Rural	49	24	25
	Urban	46	28	18
46. Saora, Savar, Saura, Sahara	Total	3,941	1,989	1,952
	Rural	3,930	1,981	1,949
	Urban	11	8	3
47. Shabar, Lodha	Total	790	423	367
	Rural	789	422	367
	Urban	1	1	0
48. Sounti	Total	1	1	0
	Rural	1	1	0
49. Tharua	Total	24	3	21
	Rural	24	3	21
50. Unclassified	Total	3	2	1
	Rural	3	2	1

Note: 1. All Scheduled Tribes includes figures for 'unclassified'.
2. Tribes having nil return are not shown.

PURI
(Undivided)

District 1	*Total/ Rural/ Urban* 2	*Population* *Total* 3	*Males* 4	*Females* 5
All Scheduled Tribes				
	Total	1,27,347	65,193	62,154
	Rural	1,07,931	54,207	53,724
	Urban	19,416	10,986	8,430
1. Bagata				
	Total	23	22	1
	Rural	12	11	1
	Urban	11	11	0
2. Baiga				
	Total	15	15	0
	Rural	12	12	0
	Urban	3	3	0
3. Banjara, Banjari				
	Total	1	1	0
	Urban	1	1	0
4. Bathudi				
	Total	326	208	118
	Rural	29	7	22
	Urban	297	201	96
5. Bhottada, Dhotada				
	Total	138	90	48
	Rural	135	87	48
	Urban	3	3	0

6. Bhuiya, Bhuyan	Total	976	379	597
	Rural	724	228	496
	Urban	252	151	101
7. Bhumia	Total	22	9	13
	Rural	3	1	2
	Urban	19	8	11
8. Bhumij	Total	672	398	274
	Rural	253	152	101
	Urban	419	246	173
9. Bhunjia	Total	14	4	10
	Rural	1	0	1
	Urban	13	4	9
10. Binjhal	Total	12	8	4
	Rural	9	5	4
	Urban	3	3	0
11. Birhor	Total	11	2	9
	Urban	11	2	9
12. Bondo Poraja	Total	12	2	10
	Rural	10	0	10
	Urban	2	2	0
13. Chenchu	Total	5	5	0
	Rural	4	4	0
	Urban	1	1	0

14. Dal				
	Total	9	8	1
	Urban	9	8	1
15. Desua Bhumij				
	Total	48	26	22
	Rural	41	20	21
	Urban	7	6	1
16. Dharua				
	Total	2	2	0
	Urban	2	2	0
17. Didayi				
	Total	14	5	9
	Urban	14	5	9
18. Gadaba				
	Total	44	13	31
	Rural	33	11	22
	Urban	11	2	9
19. Gandia				
	Total	6	4	2
	Rural	5	3	2
	Urban	1	1	0
20. Ghara				
	Total	73	28	45
	Rural	6	0	6
	Urban	67	28	39
21. Gond, Gondo				
	Total	889	512	377
	Rural	445	240	205
	Urban	444	272	172
22. Ho				
	Total	550	276	274
	Rural	216	74	142
	Urban	334	202	132

23. Holva				
	Total	20	18	2
	Rural	14	12	2
	Urban	6	6	0
24. Jatapu				
	Total	8	8	0
	Urban	8	8	0
25. Juang				
	Total	49	36	13
	Rural	12	12	0
	Urban	37	24	13
26. Kandha Gauda				
	Total	2,009	1,027	982
	Rural	1,954	1,004	950
	Urban	55	23	32
27. Kawar				
	Total	143	83	60
	Rural	106	66	40
	Urban	37	17	20
28. Kharia, Kharian				
	Total	593	328	265
	Rural	449	242	207
	Urban	144	86	58
29. Kharwar				
	Total	95	72	23
	Rural	55	45	10
	Urban	40	27	13
30. Khond, Kond, Kandha, Nanguli Kandha, Sitha Kandha				
	Total	41,707	20,730	20,977
	Rural	39,184	19,269	19,915
	Urban	2,523	1,461	1,062

31. Kisan

Total	300	200	100
Rural	96	74	22
Urban	204	126	78

32. Kol

Total	116	40	76
Rural	75	21	54
Urban	41	19	22

33. Kolah Loharas, Kol Loharas

Total	110	67	43
Rural	82	45	37
Urban	28	22	6

34. Kolha

Total	1,371	726	645
Rural	637	329	308
Urban	734	397	337

35. Koli, Malhar

Total	50	4	46
Rural	48	2	46
Urban	2	2	0

36. Kondadora

Total	68	12	56
Rural	36	4	32
Urban	32	8	24

37. Kora

Total	37	23	14
Rural	4	3	1
Urban	33	20	13

38. Korua

Total	27	15	12
Rural	23	11	12
Urban	4	4	0

39. Kotia	Total	29	28	1
	Rural	28	27	1
	Urban	1	1	0
40. Koya	Total	80	53	27
	Rural	8	8	0
	Urban	72	45	27
41. Kulis	Total	21	17	4
	Rural	1	1	0
	Urban	20	16	4
42. Lodha	Total	791	289	502
	Rural	782	281	501
	Urban	9	8	1
43. Madia	Total	111	51	60
	Rural	42	22	20
	Urban	69	29	40
44. Mahali	Total	121	62	59
	Rural	55	32	23
	Urban	66	30	36
45. Matya	Total	1,040	541	499
	Rural	835	453	382
	Urban	205	88	117
46. Mirdhas	Total	79	21	58
	Rural	45	7	38
	Urban	34	14	20

47. Munda, Munda Lohara, Munda Mahalis

	Total	4,232	2,342	1,890
	Rural	2,409	1,279	1,130
	Urban	1,823	1,063	760

48. Mundari

	Total	485	212	273
	Rural	321	123	198
	Urban	164	89	75

49. Omanatya

	Total	83	47	36
	Rural	41	24	17
	Urban	42	23	19

50. Oraon

	Total	341	167	174
	Rural	9	7	2
	Urban	332	160	172

51. Parenga

	Total	10	10	0
	Rural	10	10	0

52. Paroja

	Total	759	363	396
	Rural	630	291	339
	Urban	129	72	57

53. Pentia

	Total	46	29	17
	Rural	12	12	0
	Urban	34	17	17

54. Santal

	Total	6,274	3,600	2,674
	Rural	977	498	479
	Urban	5,297	3,102	2,195

55. Saora, Savar, Saura, Sahara				
	Total	38,266	19,711	18,555
	Rural	36,091	18,442	17,649
	Urban	2,175	1,269	906
56. Shabar, Lodha				
	Total	21,723	11,209	10,514
	Rural	18,669	9,691	8,978
	Urban	3,054	1,518	1,536
57. Sounti				
	Total	2,269	1,014	1,255
	Rural	2,240	993	1,247
	Urban	29	21	8
58. Tharua				
	Total	19	19	0
	Rural	11	11	0
	Urban	8	8	0
59. Unclassified				
	Total	3	2	1
	Rural	2	1	1
	Urban	1	1	0

Note: 1. All Scheduled Tribes includes figures for 'unclassified'.
2. Tribes having nil return are not shown.

SAMBALPUR
(Undivided)

District	*Total/ Rural/ Urban*	*Population*		
		Total	*Males*	*Females*
1	*2*	*3*	*4*	*5*
All Scheduled Tribes				
	Total	7,40,323	3,71,885	3,68,438
	Rural	6,79,930	3,40,845	3,39,085
	Urban	60,393	31,040	29,353
1. Bagata				
	Total	310	180	130
	Rural	303	174	129
	Urban	7	6	1
2. Baiga				
	Total	187	93	94
	Rural	178	84	94
	Urban	9	9	0
3. Banjara, Banjari				
	Total	2,800	1,283	1,517
	Rural	2,765	1,265	1,500
	Urban	35	18	17
4. Bathudi				
	Total	356	193	163
	Rural	46	37	9
	Urban	310	156	154
5. Bhottada, Dhotada				
	Total	90	29	61
	Rural	67	29	38
	Urban	23	0	23

6. Bhuiya, Bhuyan				
	Total	30,562	15,308	15,254
	Rural	26,568	13,282	13,286
	Urban	3,994	2,026	1,968
7. Bhumia				
	Total	95	16	79
	Rural	11	1	10
	Urban	84	15	69
8. Bhumij				
	Total	270	172	98
	Rural	143	91	52
	Urban	127	81	46
9. Bhunjia				
	Total	130	59	71
	Rural	128	57	71
	Urban	2	2	0
10. Binjhal				
	Total	74,591	38,144	36,447
	Rural	62,893	32,209	30,684
	Urban	11,698	5,935	5,763
11. Binjhia, Binjhoa				
	Total	263	110	153
	Rural	239	109	130
	Urban	24	1	23
12. Birhor				
	Total	243	104	139
	Rural	227	104	123
	Urban	16	0	16
13. Bondo Poraja				
	Total	75	31	44
	Rural	72	29	43
	Urban	3	2	1

14. Chenchu				
	Total	36	28	8
	Rural	35	27	8
	Urban	1	1	0
15. Dal				
	Total	132	62	70
	Rural	117	55	62
	Urban	15	7	8
16. Desua Bhumij				
	Total	362	183	179
	Rural	357	180	177
	Urban	5	3	2
17. Dharua				
	Total	74	52	22
	Rural	64	50	14
	Urban	10	2	8
18. Gadaba				
	Total	69	32	37
	Rural	42	20	22
	Urban	27	12	15
19. Gandia				
	Total	206	121	85
	Rural	159	93	66
	Urban	47	28	19
20. Ghara				
	Total	245	96	149
	Rural	163	75	88
	Urban	82	21	61
21. Gond, Gondo				
	Total	1,35,435	67,412	68,023
	Rural	1,26,860	62,866	63,994
	Urban	8,575	4,546	4,029

22. Ho				
	Total	1,840	1,057	783
	Rural	1,734	986	748
	Urban	106	71	35
23. Holva				
	Total	124	51	73
	Rural	106	48	58
	Urban	18	3	15
24. Jatapu				
	Total	516	277	239
	Rural	467	241	226
	Urban	49	36	13
25. Juang				
	Total	129	68	61
	Rural	120	61	59
	Urban	9	7	2
26. Kandha Gauda				
	Total	784	462	322
	Rural	701	420	281
	Urban	83	42	41
27. Kawar				
	Total	1,519	761	758
	Rural	1,477	734	743
	Urban	42	27	15
28. Kharia, Kharian				
	Total	37,352	18,381	18,971
	Rural	33,210	16,282	16,928
	Urban	4,142	2,099	2,043
29. Kharwar				
	Total	123	54	69
	Rural	116	47	69
	Urban	7	7	0

30. Khond, Kond, Kandha, Nanguli Kandha, Sitha Kandha

Total	43,654	21,972	21,682
Rural	41,324	20,670	20,654
Urban	2,330	1,302	1,028

31. Kisan

Total	1,36,902	69,232	67,670
Rural	1,27,292	64,095	63,197
Urban	9,610	5,137	4,473

32. Kol

Total	794	371	423
Rural	730	347	383
Urban	64	24	40

33. Kolah Loharas, Kol Loharas

Total	971	511	460
Rural	902	476	426
Urban	69	35	34

34. Kolha

Total	3,646	1,820	1,826
Rural	3,077	1,476	1,601
Urban	569	344	225

35. Koli, Malhar

Total	1,759	867	892
Rural	1,690	838	852
Urban	69	29	40

36. Kondadora

Total	98	57	41
Rural	65	50	15
Urban	33	7	26

37. Kora

Total	1,234	696	538
Rural	1,209	680	529
Urban	25	16	9

38. Korua				
	Total	527	274	253
	Rural	497	269	228
	Urban	30	5	25
39. Kotia				
	Total	169	102	67
	Rural	159	92	67
	Urban	10	10	0
40. Koya				
	Total	45	3	42
	Rural	45	3	42
41. Kulis				
	Total	4,630	2,363	2,267
	Rural	4,127	2,147	1,980
	Urban	503	216	287
42. Lodha				
	Total	399	192	207
	Rural	352	173	179
	Urban	47	19	28
43. Madia				
	Total	286	120	166
	Rural	250	107	143
	Urban	36	13	23
44. Mahali				
	Total	469	213	256
	Rural	411	173	238
	Urban	58	40	18
45. Mankirdia				
	Total	121	44	77
	Rural	121	44	77

46. Matya				
	Total	155	50	105
	Rural	126	38	88
	Urban	29	12	17
47. Mirdhas				
	Total	20,294	10,520	9,774
	Rural	19,352	9,980	9,372
	Urban	942	540	402
48. Munda, Munda Lohara, Munda Mahalis				
	Total	66,431	33,112	33,319
	Rural	65,430	32,640	32,790
	Urban	1,001	472	529
49. Mundari				
	Total	1,764	855	909
	Rural	1,606	784	822
	Urban	158	71	87
50. Omanatya				
	Total	319	186	133
	Rural	189	97	92
	Urban	130	89	41
51. Oraon				
	Total	35,324	17,120	18,204
	Rural	26,712	13,120	13,592
	Urban	8,612	4,000	4,612
52. Parenga				
	Total	301	122	179
	Rural	290	121	169
	Urban	11	1	10
53. Paroja				
	Total	145	95	50
	Rural	114	64	50
	Urban	31	31	0

54. Pentia				
	Total	354	212	142
	Rural	311	188	123
	Urban	43	24	19
55. Rajuar				
	Total	127	62	65
	Rural	95	42	53
	Urban	32	20	12
56. Santal				
	Total	1,249	664	585
	Rural	625	279	346
	Urban	624	385	239
57. Saora, Savar, Saura, Sahara				
	Total	1,18,956	59,983	58,973
	Rural	1,15,270	57,972	57,298
	Urban	3,686	2,011	1,675
58. Shabar, Lodha				
	Total	9,667	4,903	4,764
	Rural	7,687	3,959	3,728
	Urban	1,980	944	1,036
59. Sounti				
	Total	214	88	126
	Rural	199	83	116
	Urban	15	5	10
60. Tharua				
	Total	401	257	144
	Rural	305	182	123
	Urban	96	75	21

Note: 1. All Scheduled Tribes includes figures for 'unclassified'.
2. Tribes having nil return are not shown.

SUNDARGARH
(Undivided)

District	*Total/ Rural/ Urban*	*Population*		
		Total	*Males*	*Females*
1	*2*	*3*	*4*	*5*
All Scheduled Tribes				
	Total	7,98,481	4,00,127	3,98,354
	Rural	6,92,200	3,45,604	3,46,596
	Urban	1,06,281	54,523	51,758
1. Bagata				
	Total	2,748	1,382	1,366
	Rural	2,651	1,331	1,320
	Urban	97	51	46
2. Baiga				
	Total	150	32	118
	Rural	116	19	97
	Urban	34	13	21
3. Banjara, Banjari				
	Total	201	71	130
	Rural	171	53	118
	Urban	30	18	12
4. Bathudi				
	Total	148	81	67
	Rural	92	54	38
	Urban	56	27	29
5. Bhottada, Dhotada				
	Total	145	50	95
	Rural	99	27	72
	Urban	46	23	23

6. Bhuiya, Bhuyan	Total	77,100	39,230	37,870
	Rural	73,446	37,292	36,154
	Urban	3,654	1,938	1,716
7. Bhumia	Total	121	92	29
	Rural	85	56	29
	Urban	36	36	0
8. Bhumij	Total	5,444	2,652	2,792
	Rural	3,612	1,781	1,831
	Urban	1,832	871	961
9. Bhunjia	Total	257	135	122
	Rural	221	120	101
	Urban	36	15	21
10. Binjhal	Total	1,334	847	487
	Rural	1,105	706	399
	Urban	229	141	88
11. Binjhia, Binjhoa	Total	7,103	3,543	3,560
	Rural	6,102	3,103	2,999
	Urban	1,001	440	561
12. Bondo Poraja	Total	32	11	21
	Rural	32	11	21
13. Chenchu	Total	9	8	1
	Rural	2	1	1
	Urban	7	7	0

14. Dal

Total	14	5	9
Rural	10	1	9
Urban	4	4	0

15. Desua Bhumij

Total	71	38	33
Rural	60	38	22
Urban	11	0	11

16. Dharua

Total	30	24	6
Rural	7	7	0
Urban	23	17	6

17. Didayi

Total	5	4	1
Urban	5	4	1

18. Gadaba

Total	34	34	0
Rural	11	11	0
Urban	23	23	0

19. Gandia

Total	34	27	7
Rural	19	13	6
Urban	15	14	1

20. Ghara

Total	89	47	42
Rural	63	27	36
Urban	26	20	6

21. Gond, Gondo

Total	45,378	22,983	22,395
Rural	42,956	21,841	21,115
Urban	2,422	1,142	1,280

22. Ho	Total	2,099	1,232	867
	Rural	1,311	712	599
	Urban	788	520	268
23. Holva	Total	338	141	197
	Rural	247	104	143
	Urban	91	37	54
24. Jatapu	Total	233	140	93
	Rural	123	76	47
	Urban	110	64	46
25. Juang	Total	211	133	78
	Rural	154	95	59
	Urban	57	38	19
26. Kandha Gauda	Total	1,225	643	582
	Rural	1,065	574	491
	Urban	160	69	91
27. Kawar	Total	5,224	2,505	2,719
	Rural	5,127	2,460	2,667
	Urban	97	45	52
28. Kharia, Kharian	Total	1,05,099	51,054	54,045
	Rural	93,957	45,707	48,250
	Urban	11,142	5,347	5,795
29. Kharwar	Total	1,018	456	562
	Rural	868	374	494
	Urban	150	82	68

30. Khond, Kond, Kandha, Nanguli Kandha, Sitha Kandha

Total	3,573	2,053	1,520
Rural	3,055	1,812	1,243
Urban	518	241	277

31. Kisan

Total	1,11,206	54,647	56,559
Rural	1,01,692	49,783	51,909
Urban	9,514	4,864	4,650

32. Kol

Total	1,751	856	895
Rural	1,159	582	577
Urban	592	274	318

33. Kolah Loharas, Kol Loharas

Total	2,579	1,163	1,416
Rural	2,118	940	1,178
Urban	461	223	238

34. Kolha

Total	4,681	2,571	2,110
Rural	4,195	2,294	1,901
Urban	486	277	209

35. Koli, Malhar

Total	113	40	73
Rural	74	33	41
Urban	39	7	32

36. Kondadora

Total	113	61	52
Rural	112	61	51
Urban	1	0	1

37. Kora

Total	94	60	34
Rural	52	37	15
Urban	42	23	19

38. Korua				
	Total	528	259	269
	Rural	470	227	243
	Urban	58	32	26
39. Kotia				
	Total	37	26	11
	Rural	21	21	0
	Urban	16	5	11
40. Koya				
	Total	31	12	19
	Rural	1	1	0
	Urban	30	11	19
41. Kulis				
	Total	12	1	11
	Rural	10	0	10
	Urban	2	1	1
42. Lodha				
	Total	172	66	106
	Rural	51	27	24
	Urban	121	39	82
43. Madia				
	Total	10	9	1
	Urban	10	9	1
44. Mahali				
	Total	3,788	1,841	1,947
	Rural	2,824	1,412	1,412
	Urban	964	429	535
45. Mankidi				
	Total	48	36	12
	Rural	13	12	1
	Urban	35	24	11
46. Mankirdia				
	Total	105	52	53
	Rural	92	51	41
	Urban	13	1	12

47. Matya				
	Total	29	12	17
	Rural	9	1	8
	Urban	20	11	9
48. Mirdhas				
	Total	80	67	13
	Rural	71	66	5
	Urban	9	1	8
49. Munda, Munda Lohara, Munda Mahalis				
	Total	1,64,765	83,795	80,970
	Rural	1,35,734	68,997	66,737
	Urban	29,031	14,798	14,233
50. Mundari				
	Total	16,997	8,545	8,452
	Rural	13,364	6,467	6,897
	Urban	3,633	2,078	1,555
51. Omanatya				
	Total	247	127	120
	Rural	220	116	104
	Urban	27	11	16
52. Oraon				
	Total	2,10,004	1,04,371	1,05,633
	Rural	1,80,680	89,395	91,285
	Urban	29,324	14,976	14,348
53. Parenga				
	Total	63	48	15
	Rural	62	48	14
	Urban	1	0	1
54. Paroja				
	Total	669	340	329
	Rural	554	281	273
	Urban	115	59	56
55. Pentia				
	Total	394	221	173
	Rural	318	204	114
	Urban	76	17	59

56. Rajuar				
	Total	96	55	41
	Rural	27	15	12
	Urban	69	40	29
57. Santal				
	Total	7,121	3,979	3,142
	Rural	2,617	1,381	1,236
	Urban	4,504	2,598	1,906
58. Saora, Savar, Saura, Sahara				
	Total	2,291	1,259	1,032
	Rural	1,933	1,048	885
	Urban	358	211	147
59. Shabar, Lodha				
	Total	1,023	531	492
	Rural	882	468	414
	Urban	141	63	78
60. Sounti				
	Total	38	34	4
	Rural	32	28	4
	Urban	6	6	0
61. Tharua				
	Total	46	35	11
	Rural	40	29	11
	Urban	6	6	0
62. Unclassified				
	Total	9,883	5,355	4,528
	Rural	6,006	3,173	2,833
	Urban	3,877	2,182	1,695

Note: 1. All Scheduled Tribes includes figures for 'unclassified'.
2. Tribes having nil return are not shown.

BIBLIOGRAPHY

Bose, Ashish et al. (1990), *Demography of Tribal Development*. B. R. Publishing Corporation, New Delhi.

Bailey, FG. (1960), *Tribe Caste and Nation*. Manchester University Press, Oxford Road, Manchester, 13.

Chambers, C (1993) *Challenging the Professions*. London, Intermediate Technology Publications.

Chambers, R. (1983), *Rural Development: Putting the Last First*. Longman Scientific and Technical, Longman House, Burnt Mill, Harlaw, Essex.

Dube, SC (ed.) (1977), *The Tribal Heritage of India, Vol. 1 Ethnicity, Identity and Interaction*. Vikas Publishing House, New Delhi.

Edwards,M and Hulme, D (eds) (1993) *Making a Difference*. London, Earth Scan Publication.

Farrington, J and Lewis,D (eds) (1993) *NGOs and the State in Asia*. London, Routeledge.

Farrington J and Bebbington A (eds) (1993), *Reluctant Partners*. London and New York, Routledge.

Fernandes, Walter et al. (1989), *Development, Displacement and Rehabilitation*. Indian Social Institute, New Delhi, Mayur Enterprisers, New Delhi.

Furer-Haimendorf, V. (1982), *The Tribes of India*. University of California Press, Berkelay, Los Angeles and London.

Fuchs, S. (1977), *The Aboriginal Tribes of India*. The Mac Millan Press Limited, London and Basing Stoke. 9. 9. 8.

Ghurye, GS. (1959), *The Scheduled Tribe*. Popular Book Depot, Bombay.

Gomango, G. (1992), *Constitutional Provisions for the Scheduled Castes and Scheduled Tribes*. Himalaya Publishing House, Bombay, Delhi, Nagpur.

Human Development Report (1993). Published by UNDP, Delhi. Oxford University Press, Bombay, Madras, Calcutta.

Jones, JHM. (1994), *Changing Patterns of Informal and Formal Finance in a Rajasthan Village*. Ph.D. Thesis, Reading University.

Naik, TB.(1984), "What is a Tribe: Conflicting and Deflecting" in Vidyarthy, LP.(ed.) *Applied Anthropology in India*. (Second Edition) Kitab Mahal, Allahabad.

Poulton, R. and Harris, M (eds) (1988) *Putting People First: Voluntary Organisations and Third World Organisations*. London and Basingstoke, Macmillan Publishers.

Robinson, MA (1991) *Evaluating the impact of NGOs in rural poverty alleviation: India Country Study*. London, Overseas Development Study.

Roy, S (1989) *"The Tilonia Movement; Profile of an Alternative Approach" Strategic Issues in Development Management: Learning from Successful Experiences* (253-273) London, Commonwealth Secretariat.

Srinivas, MN. (1966), *Caste and Change in Modern India*. California University Press, Berkeley and California.

Taradatt (1995), *Tribal Education in Orissa*. Orissa Review, Bhubaneswar.

Valley, P (1990) *Bad Samaritans*. London Sydney Auckland Toronto, Hodder and Stoughton Ltd.

Verrier, E. (1964), *The Tribal World of Verrier Elwin*. Oxford University Press, Amen House, London.

Verrier, E. (1939), *The Vaiga*. John Murray, Albe Marle Street, West London.

White S, Sarah (1991) *Evaluating the Impact of NGOs in Rural Poverty Alleviation: Bengladesh Country Study*. London, Overseas Development Institute.

Agriculture Census Commissioner, Board of Revenue, Orissa (1985-86), *Report on the Number and area of Operational Holdings in Orissa* (Agriculture census Report). Cuttack.

Commissioner for Scheduled Castes and Scheduled Tribes (1990), *Twenty-ninth Report*, 1987-89. New Delhi.

Directorate of Agriculture and Food production, Orissa (1993), *Orissa Agricultural Statistics*, 1990-91. Bhubaneswar.

Directorate of Economics and Statistics, Orissa (1991), *Statistical Abstract, 1991*. Bhubaneswar.

Government of India, Ministry of Home Affairs (1960), *Report of the Committee on Special Multipurpose Tribal Blocks*. New Delhi.

Government of India (1960-61), *Report of Scheduled Areas and*

Scheduled Tribes Commission. New Delhi.

Government of India (1969), *Report of the Study Team Tribal Development programme* on . New Delhi.

Government of India, Ministry of Home Affairs (1978), *Report of Study group on Administrative Arrangements and Personnel Policies in Tribal Areas*. New Delhi.

Government of India, Ministry of Home Affairs (1980), *Tribal Development in Fifth Plan, some basic Policy Papers, Vol. I & II* New Delhi.

Government of India, Ministry of Home Affairs (1980), *Report of the Working Group on Tribal Development during Sixth Five Year Plan*, 1980-85. New Delhi.

Government of India, Ministry of Rural Development (January, 1995), *Report of the Committee of Members of Parliament and Experts Constituted to make Recommendations on law Concerning Extentsion of Provision of the Constitution (seventy-third Amendment) act, 1992 to Scheduled Areas*, New Delhi.

Government of India, Ministry of Home Affairs (1984), *Report of the Working Group on Development of Scheduled Tribes during Seventh Five Year Plan*, 1985-90. New Delhi.

Government of India, Ministry of Welfare (1989), *Report of the Working Group on Development and Welfare of Scheduled Tribes during Eighth Five Year Plan*, 1990-95. New Delhi.

Government of Orissa, Harijan and Tribal Welfare Department (1991), *Tribal Sub Plan for Eighth Plan, 1992-97 and Annual Plan 1992-93*. Bhubaneswar.

Government of Orissa, Harijan and Tribal Welfare Department, Bhubneswar, (1990), *Tribes of Orissa*.

Government of Orissa, State Planning Machinery, Planning and Coordination Department (1988), *Indicators of Economic Development of Orrissa 1980-81 to 1983-84*. Bhubaneswar.

Government of Orissa, Department of Education (1992), *Discussion Paper on South Orissa Education Project*. Bhubaneswar.

National Committee on the Development of Backward Areas (1981), *Report on Development of Tribal Areas*. Planning Commission, Government of India, New Delhi.

Registrar General of India, *Census Report, 1991*, New Delhi.

Index

U

V